LIVNOT

A Biblical Framework to Build, Rebuild, Construct & Establish

Mitul Parivah

LIVNOT
A Biblical Framework to Build, Rebuild, Construct & Establish

Paperback Edition
ISBN: 978-93-5619-577-6
First Edition: 2025
Published by: Mitul Parivah
Imprint: Independently published
Cover design & interior formatting: ***maxify prints***

DEDICATION

To my Spiritual Parents,

Apostle Dr. Alph Lukau
&
Bishop Celeste Lukau

CONTENTS

ACKNOWLEDGMENTS

I thank my Heavenly Father, who chose me from my mother's womb for His glory. I am deeply grateful to the Lord Jesus Christ for His grace through which I am redeemed, and to the Holy Spirit for His revelation and continuous guidance in my life.

I sincerely thank Dad Apostle Dr. Alph Lukau and Mom Celeste Lukau, who remain on their knees so that we may stand on our feet. My heartfelt gratitude also goes to all the bishops—Bishop Jacky, Bishop Shepherd Gwenzi, and Bishop Stephane Aduya—as well as all the pastors and ministers who faithfully serve.

I am especially thankful to the AMI media team for their tireless efforts in bringing the altar of AMI directly to my screen. Though I have not yet been physically present at the altar, I feel deeply connected to the entire AMI family—from AMI Praise and ushers to the disciples and every member serving faithfully.

Together for life.

Introduction

Hello, dear reader.
Before we dive into the chapters of this book, let us first understand its name: **LIVNOT**.

The Hebrew word **LIVNOT (לִבְנוֹת)** means "*to build*" or "*to construct.*" It is used in the Bible for building houses, cities, altars, and temples. It comes from the same root as **banah (בָּנָה)**, a common biblical word meaning *to build*. But LIVNOT is not limited to physical structures. It is also used in a deeper, symbolic sense—to build a family, a nation, a future, or a spiritual life.

LIVNOT is more than a word; it is a picture. In Scripture, *to build* often means partnering with God in restoration, growth, and establishment. It speaks of seasons when God invites His people not just to survive hardship, but to rise and build something lasting according to His will.

There is another Hebrew concept closely connected to this idea: **Chochmah**, which means wisdom. Chochmah is like a flash of insight—the seed of an idea. **Binah (בִּינָה)** is the ability to take that seed and develop it, giving it structure and form. In simple terms, LIVNOT is what happens when wisdom moves from idea to action—when what God reveals begins to take shape in real life.

As a spiritual son of **Apostle Dr. Alph Lukau**, I

wrote this book in the context of our prophetic theme: "**2026 – The Year to Build, Rebuild, Construct, and Establish.**" The word **LIVNOT** *[pronounced leev-NOHT, with the emphasis on the last syllable]* appears many times in the Torah, the Old Testament of the Bible. It is most often used to describe the building or rebuilding of the house of God. We see this during the time of King Solomon, when the Temple was built (1 Kings 5:19; 2 Chronicles 2:4; 2 Chronicles 3:1). Later, after the exile, the same word is used in the books of Ezra, where the Temple of God and the walls of Jerusalem were rebuilt (Ezra 1:2; Ezra 1:5; Ezra 4:3). The prophet Jeremiah also uses this language when God speaks of rebuilding and planting the nation once again.

In the New Covenant, the idea of building takes on a deeper meaning. Jesus said in **John 2:19**, "*Destroy this temple, and in three days I will raise it up.*" He was speaking about the temple of His body. Later, Scripture explains this truth even further. **Ephesians 2:21–22** says that "*In whom the whole building, being joined together, grows into a holy temple in the Lord, in whom you also are being built together for a dwelling place of God in the Spirit.*" This means that believers themselves are now the true temple of God. The greatest construction project is no longer made of stone, but of lives transformed by Christ.

Ecclesiastes 3:3 tells us there is "*a time to break down, and **a time to build (livnot).***" In everyday life, this speaks to seasons when God releases grace to build the right mindset, flourishing relationships, a healthy and debt-free financial life, and systems. In this book, *building* applies to very practical areas: building a career, rebuilding broken relationships, constructing a meaningful life, and establishing God's Kingdom in every area—work, finances, family, emotions, and faith that reflect **ZOE—the God-kind of life**, where *nothing is broken and nothing is missing*.

This is a self-help book, but from a biblical standpoint. It is a practical guide to everyday life, rooted in Scripture and guided by the Spirit of God. The principles here help you move from merely coping with life to intentionally building what God desires.

In 2022, I reached the lowest point of my life. Living with an incurable disease (which surely will be curable for God's glory), bound to a wheelchair, I saw no clear way forward. I faced a painful financial betrayal that left me in heavy debt. Another trusted friend walked away, leaving me feeling abandoned, physically broken (due to fracture in hip-ball), emotionally exhausted, and spiritually wounded. My life felt shattered into pieces, and I did not know how to rebuild it.

Over the next few years, God led me through a rebuilding process. I learned how to handle setbacks, recover from emotional trauma, regain discipline, clear debt, and rediscover purpose. Looking back, I now understand the saying: "*Every glory has a story.*" This book is not about my story—it is about the **process** and **principles** that helped me rebuild my life. Along the way, I read so many self-help books, attended a few online programs and lots of growth oriented content. I realized that many self-help methods used around the world are actually rooted in biblical truths & Spiritual principles even when Scripture is not acknowledged.

What you hold in your hands is the result of lessons learned through pain, wisdom received from God, and truth tested in real life. This book is my small way of helping those who are ready to claim what is rightfully theirs according to **Ephesians 1:3** and who desire to build something solid in alignment with the prophetic theme of 2026 and beyond.

If you are willing to **build**, **rebuild**, **construct**, and **establish**—a Christ-centered life—then let us begin this journey together.

Welcome to **LIVNOT**.

Chapter 1

The Christian Life of Purpose

God Gives Everyone a Purpose

From the very beginning, God has always acted with purpose. He never created anyone without a plan. Throughout the Bible, from the Old Testament to the New, every person God called was chosen for a reason, and their lives played a part in His bigger plan. God designs each life for a special role. No calling is random, and every person's life has meaning in God's Kingdom.

Adam was appointed by God to care for and rule over creation **(Genesis 1:28)**. Noah was chosen to build the ark and save life during the flood **(Genesis 6:13-22)**. Abraham was called to leave his homeland and become the father of many nations **(Genesis 12:1-3)**.

Moses, who grew up in Pharaoh's palace, was called to deliver Israel from slavery (Exodus 3:10). David started as a shepherd boy but was anointed to become the king of Israel (1 Samuel 16:12-13). Daniel, even while living in exile, was given wisdom and excellence to influence kings and kingdoms (Daniel 1:17-21).

In the New Testament, God called Peter, a fisherman, to become a shepherd and leader of the early Church (John 21:15-17). Paul, who once persecuted Christians, was chosen to preach the Gospel to the Gentiles (Acts 9:15).

"The Lord has called Me from the womb; From the matrix of My mother, He has made mention of My name." — ***Isaiah 49:1 (NKJV)***

God's purpose for our lives begins even before we are born. He knows us by name and has already planned something special for us.

"Before I formed you in the womb I knew you; Before you were born I sanctified you; I ordained you a prophet to the nations." — ***Jeremiah 1:5 (NKJV)***

Jeremiah was not just born to live—he was born with a prophetic purpose. The same truth applies to each of us.

Paul writes to Timothy:

"[God] has saved us and called us with a holy calling, not according to our works, but according to His own purpose and grace which was given to us in Christ Jesus before time began." — ***2 Timothy 1:9 (NKJV)***

Every believer has a holy calling—not because of what we have done, but because of God's purpose and grace.

You are not on this earth by accident. Every person is created by God with a purpose, and **no one is jobless in the Kingdom of God**. Each of us is uniquely equipped with gifts, talents, and skills—not for our own benefit alone, but to fulfil a God-given mission. As the Bible says:

"For we are His workmanship, created in Christ Jesus for good works, which God prepared beforehand that we should walk in them." — ***Ephesians 2:10 (NKJV)***

Just like Adam, Noah, Moses, and Paul, your life carries a specific assignment from God. The key is to seek Him, understand your purpose, and walk in it by faith. You are **called, chosen, and commissioned** for something greater than just existing. God is waiting for you to discover, embrace, and act on that unique calling.

We are not here just to survive, pass time, or live aimlessly. Every believer has been **carefully designed** to make a difference. Your purpose matters. Your life matters.

We All Have Different Roles

God has called each of us for a purpose, but our roles are not all the same. Just like a human body has many different parts such as hands, feet, eyes, and ears. And each part has its own job. In the same way, the Body of Christ, which is the Church, is made up of many people, each with a unique role to play. The Bible teaches this clearly in **1 Corinthians 12:12–27**. The Apostle Paul uses the example of the human body to explain how the Church works. He says:

"For as the body is one and has many members, but all the members of that one body, being many, are one body, so also is Christ... but now indeed there are many members, yet one body." — ***1 Corinthians 12:12, 20***

Every believer is important, no matter what their role is. Some may serve in visible positions, and others may work quietly behind the scenes—but all are needed. No one is greater or lesser, and no one is left out or without purpose. God has placed each of us where we are for a reason. Whether your role is inside the church or in your everyday life, it is valuable. When we understand our role and work together in unity, we reflect the beauty and power of Christ's body working in harmony—all for the glory of God.

In the Church, God has given different spiritual responsibilities to different people. As it says:

"And He Himself gave some to be apostles, some prophets, some evangelists, and some pastors and teachers." — ***Ephesians 4:11***

These are leadership roles, and they play a vital part in guiding and building the Church. However, leadership is not the only way to serve. There are many other roles in the Church that may seem small but are equally important and valuable. Some people serve as **ushers**, helping to welcome and guide others. Some are part of the **praise and worship team**, leading the congregation into God's presence through music. Others serve in the **intercessory department**, praying faithfully for the needs of the Church.

Some are involved in **administration and management**, ensuring that everything runs smoothly. Today, with modern technology, many serve in the **media team**, helping with livestreaming, audio-visuals, and designing graphics for church services and online ministry.

And last but not least, there are the **kingdom financiers,** those whom God has blessed financially and who help to advance the Kingdom through their giving.

In Personal Life, our calling is not limited to church activities. God has also given each of us a mission outside the church walls. Not everyone is called to preach from a pulpit or lead worship on stage. In fact, most believers are called to serve and shine in their everyday lives like at their jobs, in their schools, and within their communities.

Some people work in banks, others run businesses. Some are nurses, teachers, engineers, artists, or students. Wherever God has placed you, that place is your mission field. You can honour God by working with excellence, showing kindness, and sharing His love with those around you.

The Bible reminds us that these different callings are all part of God's big plan. Each person brings something valuable. You might be the only believer your coworkers or classmates ever meet. God can use you right where you are to encourage, to preach the gospel, and be a light in your workplace, classroom, or home.

No matter the role, each one plays a key part in building up the Church and bringing people closer to God. Every task, whether seen or unseen, is important in God's eyes.

The Twelve Tribes

In the Old Testament, the twelve tribes of Israel show us a powerful truth: **diversity creates perfection**. Each tribe had a unique role, yet all were part of God's bigger plan. If everyone had served in the temple, then who would have brought the offerings or provided the materials needed for worship? God, in His wisdom, assigned different tasks to different tribes, and each one was important.

The **tribe of Levi** was set apart to serve in the Tabernacle. They were responsible for its care and spiritual duties (Numbers 1:50–53; 3:5–10; Deuteronomy 10:8). Even within Levi, there were special roles—**Kohathites** carried holy items, **Gershonites** managed the coverings, and **Merarites** handled the structure (Numbers 4). Serving God in the temple was a demanding and holy task.

The other eleven tribes had different responsibilities. The **tribe of Judah** led in battle and leadership (Numbers 2:3–4; Genesis 49:10). **Issachar** was known for wisdom and understanding of the times (1 Chronicles 12:32). **Zebulun** focused on trade and warfare (Genesis 49:13; Deuteronomy 33:18–19), while **Dan** was linked with justice and military skill (Genesis 49:16–17). **Benjamin** was known for courage and strength in battle (Genesis 49:27). **Joseph**, through his sons **Ephraim and Manasseh**, received blessings of fruitfulness and inheritance (Genesis 49:22–26; Deuteronomy 33:13–17). These roles remind us that **not everyone is called to do the same thing**, but everyone is called to do **something meaningful**. Together, they built a strong nation and fulfilled God's will.

This idea of different callings continues in the New Testament. Jesus chose disciples from various backgrounds and professions. For instance, Peter, John, and James were fishermen. Matthew was a tax collector, and Luke was a doctor. Each one had a different skill set and calling. What this teaches us is that every believer is called to do a task that suits their gifts and background. Whether our work is in the church or in the world, we should serve wholeheartedly with the unique purpose God has given us.

The message is clear that we all are called for a specific task. Your role might be different from someone else's, but it is equally important. What matters is that we do our part wholeheartedly and faithfully. When we all serve in our unique roles, God's Kingdom grows stronger and His purpose is fulfilled on earth.

Called to Rule, Prosper, and Win

"We are here to rule until Jesus Crist returns" - ***AMI***

From the very beginning, God designed mankind not just to exist, but to **rule**, **prosper**, and **walk in victory**. We were created in God's image and likeness with a divine purpose and to govern the earth and represent His authority.

"So God created man in His own image; ***in the image of God He created him****; male and female He created them. Then God blessed them, and God said to them, 'Be fruitful and multiply; fill the earth and* ***subdue it; have dominion*** *over the fish of the sea, over the birds of the air, and over every living thing that moves on the earth.'"* — ***Genesis 1:27-28 (NKJV)***

This means we were entrusted with divine responsibility to manage the earth. To "***subdue***" is to bring order and influence, and to "***have dominion***" is to lead with authority, not through oppression, but through godly stewardship. God intended us to be solution-bringers and leaders who reflect His character on the earth.

Though the original dominion was lost due to sin, Jesus came to restore it. Through His sacrifice and resurrection, every born-again believer becomes a **partaker of divine victory**. We are no longer bound by defeat, fear, or sin. Instead, we walk in the same victory Christ won at the cross. This victory is not a lucky chance; it's part of God's deliberate plan for us to live from a position of faith, confidence, and continual growth. We are not fighting for victory; we are fighting in victory. As sons and daughters of God, we are destined to rise above every challenge and circumstance with the mindset of **'more than a conqueror' (Romans 8:37)**.

God desires wholeness and prosperity for His people **(3 John 1:2)**. This prosperity goes far beyond money, rather it includes good health, emotional strength, spiritual maturity, and fruitful work. He wants to see you thrive in your studies, career, business, relationships, and personal life. God delights in your success because it reflects His goodness. When your soul prospers, meaning when your thoughts, attitudes, and inner life are aligned with God, then everything else in your life begins to flourish. **Excellence, growth, and favour** are meant to follow those who walk with God.

We are not created to struggle at the bottom. God's promise is clear: those who walk in obedience to His

Word are called to lead, not lag behind **(Deuteronomy 28:13)**. Being the "*head and not the tail*" means taking charge, making decisions, and influencing your environment with righteousness. To be "*above only*" means that setbacks cannot define you, because God's favour always lifts you. You're not a follower of trends, someone who moves forward with divine backing. Just as **Bishop Jacky** often says, "*We are always in front, not behind.*" That is not arrogance; it's identity.

We are not orphans in the Kingdom but we are **heirs**. God owns everything: gold, silver, livestock, and every form of resource **(Haggaib2:8, Psalms 50:10)**. And He has not withheld it from His children. He gives us the **power, wisdom, and creativity** to generate wealth and make a lasting impact. As joint heirs with Christ **(Romans 8:16-17)**, we have access to heavenly abundance. This doesn't mean we chase riches for pride, it means we use resources to serve God's purpose, live with dignity, and bless others. When you understand whose child you are, you begin to see wealth not as a wish, but as a birthright **(Deuteronomy 8:18)**, used wisely and managed faithfully.

We are not called to live small, fearful lives. We are called to walk in dominion, carry divine influence, and demonstrate God's glory in all that we do. To rule means we stand firm in our spiritual authority. To prosper means we shine in every area of life, not just for ourselves, but to point others to God. And to win means we overcome every opposition, not by might, but by faith and alignment with God's plan. Your victory is not just for personal gain, rather it's part of your calling to expand the Kingdom of God on earth.

Our Identity in the New Covenant

In Christ, we are not just improved versions of our old selves, rather we are entirely new creations. Through His blood, Jesus established a New Covenant, one that surpasses the old in glory, grace, and access to God. We no longer live under the weight of the law but under the freedom of grace. Jesus became the perfect sacrifice on our behalf, paid the full price for our redemption, and ushered us into a life of purpose, authority, and intimacy with God.

When someone is truly in Christ, their old life with all its guilt, shame, fear, and separation from God, is completely erased. This isn't merely a fresh start but it's a total spiritual rebirth. You are not improved; you are made entirely new from the inside out. Your identity is no longer defined by your past mistakes, your background, or your limitations. It is defined by the finished work of Christ on the cross. You don't have to strive for God's approval; you already have it.

"Therefore, if anyone is in Christ, he is a new creation; old things have passed away; behold, all things have become new."— ***2 Corinthians 5:17 (NKJV)***

Under the Old Covenant, the people of God approached Him as servants. Distant, reverent, but without full access. But everything changed through Jesus Christ. In the New Covenant, we are no longer merely servants but we are sons and daughters of the Most High. We are adopted into God's family with full rights, privileges, and inheritance.

You no longer need a human priest or prophet as a mediator between you and God. Jesus Himself is your eternal Mediator, and through Him, you have direct access to the Father. You can speak to Him, walk with Him, and be assured that He sees you, hears you, and calls you His own.

"But as many as received Him, to them He gave the right to become children of God, to those who believe in His name."— ***John 1:12***

"For you are all sons of God through faith in Christ Jesus." — ***Galatians 3:26***

In the Old Testament, the Holy Spirit would come upon individuals temporarily, to empower them for specific missions, battles, or prophetic acts. But in the New Covenant, something extraordinary has happened: the Holy Spirit now lives within us permanently.

You are not just a follower of Christ; you are a living temple of the Holy Spirit. This means you carry God's presence wherever you go. You don't have to wait for an external move of God but God himself is moving within you. His guidance, power, and comfort are not distant; they dwell inside you. You are never alone. You are divinely equipped and continually led from within.

"Or do you not know that your body is the temple of the Holy Spirit who is in you, whom you have from God, and you are not your own?" — ***1 Corinthians 6:19***

Under the Old Covenant, only a chosen few like kings, priests, and prophets were anointed to carry divine authority or fulfill spiritual roles. Think of Saul, David, the Levite priests, and the prophets. Their calling was unique, and their access to God was limited by covenant and calling.

But now, under the New Covenant, that privilege is no longer reserved for a few. It's the inheritance of every believer. In Christ, You are royally positioned, you've been made both king and priest. As a king, you are called to reign in life with righteousness, wisdom, and authority, whereas as a priest, you have intimate access to God to worship, intercede, and minister before Him. You carry heavenly authority and priestly purpose in your daily life.

"And have made us kings and priests to our God; and we shall reign on the earth." — ***Revelation 5:10***

Jesus empowered us with authority. Not just pastors, prophets, or apostles but every believer has been entrusted with real spiritual authority. Through the name of Jesus, we are commissioned to confront darkness and establish God's kingdom on earth. You have been given divine power to cast out demons and dismantle strongholds, heal the sick and restore the broken, speak with new tongues and operate in spiritual gifts. When you speak in the name of Jesus, heaven backs you up. The forces of hell have no choice but to obey. You are not powerless, fragile, or unarmed. You are divinely equipped to bring freedom, healing, and light into the darkest places.

"And these signs will follow those who believe: In My name they will cast out demons; they will speak with new tongues; they will take up serpents; and if they drink anything deadly, it will by no means hurt them; they will lay hands on the sick, and they will recover."
— Mark 16:17–18

We are not just people on earth trying to reach heaven. We are already spiritually seated with Christ in heavenly places. This divine positioning speaks of authority, victory, and rest. It means we operate not from a place of struggle, but from a place of spiritual advantage and confidence.

"And raised us up together, and made us sit together in the heavenly places in Christ Jesus." ***— Ephesians 2:6***

From this exalted position, you're called to see your life, challenges, and future from a higher perspective. You are not fighting for blessings, rather you're living from them. You've already been given access to every spiritual blessing in Christ.

So when you pray, declare, or act in faith, you're not begging God, you're releasing what is already yours in Christ. Your identity, authority, and inheritance are secured above. You carry kingdom authority here on earth because your spirit is seated there in heaven.

"Blessed be the God and Father of our Lord Jesus Christ, who has blessed us with every spiritual blessing in the heavenly places in Christ." — ***Ephesians 1:3***

In short, we are not who the world says we are; we are who God says we are. We are not ordinary; we are sons and daughters of the King. We carry divine authority and are called to reign in life through Christ. In academics, jobs, business, and relationships, we are called to lead and shine. We don't strive for blessings; we operate from a place of victory. This is our new identity, our divine calling, and our time to make a difference.

The Importance of Spiritual and Personal Growth

Even though believers have been given great privileges, spiritual authority, and the right to succeed through Christ, many still struggle in their day-to-day lives. This is something we cannot ignore. There are Christians who feel stuck, frustrated, or unable to live the victorious life that God has promised. Why does this happen? The Bible gives us a clear and honest answer:

"My people are destroyed for lack of knowledge" - ***Hosea 4:6 (NKJV)***

It's not because God hasn't blessed them, or that they lack favor or access to His power. The problem is often a lack of understanding. Many believers don't fully know who they are in Christ, how to apply God's Word in practical life, or how to grow in wisdom and discipline. It's not enough to simply believe—we must also learn, grow, and take action. Without knowledge, people perish not because God wants them to, but because they fail to walk in what's already been given to them.

Think of it like learning to swim. Just knowing that you're allowed to swim or praying hard about it won't make you a swimmer. There are steps you need to take such as you must set a goal, join a class, learn the technique, and practice regularly. You'll face fear, fail sometimes, feel discouraged, but you must keep going. God is always there to rescue you if you're drowning. However, you cannot claim the promise that 'rivers cannot drown you.' Of course, God will rescue you in times of crisis, but that doesn't mean you will become a swimming champion just by relying on the promise. If you truly want to swim well, you have to do the work.

The same is true in life. Prayer and faith are powerful, but they don't replace action. God will empower you, guide you, and give you strength but He will not do your part. He won't study for you, build your business for you, or manage your time for you. You are the doer. His power flows through your obedience, discipline, and growth. That's how spiritual life meets real life.

That is why you must grow both spiritually and personally. Spiritually, you need to know your identity in Christ, be sensitive to the Holy Spirit, follow divine instructions, and build a strong relationship with God. This deepens your inner life and gives you wisdom and strength for any situation. You gain courage and boldness in God, along with resilience and strength to face and overcome the battles of life.

At the same time, personal growth is equally important. Learn to manage your time well, improve your communication skills, develop a strong and renewed mindset, and sharpen your approach and strategies in whatever area you are called to—whether it is business, academics, or any other field where God has placed you to make an impact.

God is a righteous judge, and He shows no partiality. For example, if a non-believer studies 12 hours a day, staying away from distractions, and a believer spends time playing games and scrolling on social media, who will score better in the exam? The one who put in the effort. God's mercy and favor are real, but they do not replace responsibility and discipline; they assist you in times of need. Favor might help you pass in a crisis, but it will not make you a topper without preparation.

I have personally seen this happen. Back in 12th grade, some of my friends believed that God would help them in exams, even though they hardly studied. As a result, they barely passed. Faith is powerful, but it must be paired with action.

So do not wait passively for breakthroughs. Grow in knowledge. Learn new skills. Apply wisdom. Walk closely with God and take responsibility for your life. That is how you rule and thrive. Today, even non-believers are achieving success by applying biblical principles through self-help and personal development. It is time for believers to rise, take hold of God's promises, and possess their promised land.

Live an Intentional Life

This book is your invitation to step into a life of purpose, clarity, and intentional living. Whether you are a student preparing for exams, a businessperson making strategic decisions, an employee working towards promotion, a home-maker managing your family, or even a pastor shepherding people—this message is for you. Living intentionally means no longer drifting through life, but waking up each day with a sense of direction and divine assignment. You will learn how to live not just reactively, but proactively—with purpose in your steps and wisdom in your choices.

Throughout this book, we will dive deep into tools and techniques that help you make the most of your time, energy, and potential. In today's world filled with non-stop notifications and distractions, focus has become a rare gift. You will discover how to regain it through proven methods like the Pomodoro Technique, which helps you stay mentally sharp and productive by working in focused bursts followed by short breaks. This simple approach can transform the way you work, study, or manage your daily responsibilities.

We often hear the verse, "Do not worry about anything," but many of us do not know how to actually stop worrying. That is why this book will also guide you through a powerful and visual exercise called The Balloon Method. It will teach you how to identify your worries, release them, and experience peace by trusting God deeply and practically.

From setting clear goals to building a step-by-step path to achieving them, we will walk through the entire process of living a fruitful life. But unlike many self-help guides, this journey is not built on human wisdom alone—it is rooted in biblical truth. God's Word offers the richest guidance for decision-making, time management, discipline, and success.

By the end of this book, you will not only know what it means to live with intention, but you will also have practical strategies to align your daily life with your divine calling. No more living aimlessly. It is time to live wisely, walk boldly, and fulfil the purpose for which you were created.

Chapter 2

The Battle of the Mind

Why Your Thoughts Matter

"Set your mind on things above, not on things on the earth." - ***Colossians 3:2***

This is not just a suggestion, it's a key principle for living a victorious and intentional life. Your mind is the steering wheel of your life. Where your thoughts go, your life follows. That's why the Bible teaches us to focus on God's truth, His promises, and the eternal perspective He gives.

In today's fast-moving world, your mind is constantly being fed through social media, news, conversations, advertisements, and even your own past experiences. Many of these messages are filled with fear, comparison, insecurity, and doubt. Over time, these thoughts become beliefs, and those beliefs shape how you see yourself and the world around you. If your mind is filled with thoughts like "I'm not good enough," "I'll never succeed," or "No one cares about me," you start living as if those things are true but they are the lies of the enemy. But God has given you a powerful truth: you are His child, created with purpose, filled with His Spirit, and seated with Christ in heavenly places. You were never meant to live small, afraid, or defeated. You were born to rule and thrive. That begins with your mind.

Think of your mind like a garden. If you plant negative, fearful, or worldly thoughts, you will grow weeds such as stress, frustration, insecurity, and confusion. But if you plant godly thoughts like "I am loved by God," "I can do all things through Christ," and "God's plans for me are good", you will see the fruit of peace, confidence, wisdom, and purpose in your life. The more you feed your mind with God's Word and truth, the more you will begin to think, speak, and act from a place of spiritual authority.

This is why it's not enough to simply go to church or say a few prayers. Your daily thought life must be aligned with God's Word. When you set your mind on heavenly things like things that are pure, loving, wise, and purposeful, you begin to live intentionally. You make better decisions in your studies, your career, your relationships, and even your habits. You start showing up with confidence in the workplace, dreaming bigger in your business, studying with discipline, and leading your family with love and clarity.

Your thoughts can either build you up or tear you down. They can either empower you to walk in the calling God has placed on your life or keep you stuck in cycles of fear and failure. But the choice is yours. Will you think like the world, or will you think like someone seated with Christ? Will you think like a slave to your past, or like a son or daughter of the King?

The Mind as a Spiritual Battleground

"But I see another law in my members, warring against the law of my mind, and bringing me into captivity to the law of sin which is in my members." - ***Romans 7:23***

These are powerful words from the Apostle Paul, one of the greatest men of God, who openly shared the inner struggle he faced. Even though he had a deep relationship with God, Paul admitted that there was a war going on inside him—a battle between the desires of the Spirit and the demands of the flesh.

This battle still exists today in every believer. Our mind is the place where this war is most intense. On one side, we have the Spirit of God leading us toward peace, obedience, purpose, and love. On the other side, our human nature—along with worldly distractions and temptations—pulls us toward fear, unforgiveness, pride, laziness, and sin.

For instance, you might know that God wants you

to forgive someone who hurt you. Deep inside, your spirit agrees with forgiveness. But your mind brings back painful memories and whispers, “They don’t deserve it.” Or maybe you want to wake up early and spend time with God, but your mind argues, “Just sleep a little more, you’re tired.” Or you decide to focus on your goals, but end up scrolling through social media for hours. These examples show us that the real struggle is not outside–it is within our minds.

This is why the Bible emphasizes the importance of **renewing your mind**. Until we win this battle in our thoughts, we cannot truly experience freedom or walk in the authority God has given us. The enemy knows that if he can control your mind, he can control your decisions and ultimately your destiny. That’s why every spiritual battle starts in the thought life.

If you keep thinking thoughts like “I can’t do it,” “I’ll always be stuck,” or “Nothing will change,” you start living according to those thoughts. But if you begin replacing those lies with truth like “I can do all things through Christ,” “God is working all things for my good,” and “I have the mind of Christ”, then you begin to take back territory in your life.

Think of your mind like a war zone. Every thought that enters is either a weapon used by the enemy to destroy your peace, purpose, and progress or a weapon used by God to build your character, courage, and calling. The choice is yours. What kind of thoughts will you entertain? What kind of thoughts will you fight with?

How Beliefs Shape Actions and Outcomes

"For as he thinks in his heart, so is he." - ***Proverbs 23:7***

This short verse holds a deep truth: your beliefs shape your identity, your decisions, and ultimately, your destiny. The thoughts you hold deep within your heart are not just silent ideas but they are the driving force behind your words, actions, habits, and even your future.

If someone believes they are weak, unworthy, or not good enough, they will carry themselves that way. They may never try to apply for a better job, speak in public, or pursue a dream. Why? Because their belief has already defeated them before they even started. On the other hand, if a person believes, "I am created in God's image, I am chosen, and with His help, I can grow," they will start to act with courage, make better choices, and move forward, even when things feel hard.

Let's take a practical example: Imagine two students preparing for an exam. One says, "I always fail in math. I'm just not smart enough." The other says, "I may struggle, but with practice and God's help, I can improve." The first student might give up quickly or study half-heartedly, while the second one is more likely to seek help, practice more, and believe for a better result. And usually, they will succeed, not because they were smarter, but because their belief moved them into action.

Beliefs are like seeds. What you plant in your mind will grow in your life. If you keep planting thoughts of fear, failure, and insecurity, don't be surprised if you see anxiety, procrastination, and broken dreams. But if you plant seeds of faith, truth, and possibility, you'll begin to see confidence, purpose, and fruitfulness grow.

Our beliefs act like the steering wheel of a car, determining the direction we move. Even if your life is filled with potential, the wrong beliefs will keep turning your wheel in the wrong direction. My spiritual father, **Apostle Dr. Alph Lukau**, says, "Direction is more important than just moving forward—if you move in the wrong direction, you will end up reaching somewhere else, not your intended destination." That's why it's so important to align your beliefs with what God says about you in His Word concerning your destiny.

So, before you begin your journey toward a purposeful and impactful life, you must first win the battle in your mind. This is where everything begins. Whether you're a student battling distraction, a professional dealing with stress, a parent managing responsibilities, or a believer struggling with doubt; your thoughts are either building your future or silently sabotaging it.

The mind is the control room of your life. If you allow fear, insecurity, or negative thinking to dominate, they will become invisible chains that hold you back. But when you take authority over your thoughts and aligning them with God's Word, you begin to live free, focused, and full of purpose.

God has not called you to just survive the war in your mind; He has called you to conquer it. And with His Spirit in you, you have everything you need to do just that. Start by identifying the wrong patterns of thinking that have kept you stuck. Break the mental strongholds that tell you "I can't," "I'm not enough," or "It's too late." Then fill your mind with truth that says, "I am loved," "I am chosen," "I am equipped," and "I am victorious through Christ."

Recognize the power of your beliefs. As Proverbs 23:7 says, "As a man thinks in his heart, so is he." You don't rise to the level of your dreams, rather you rise to the level of your beliefs. What you think today is shaping the life you'll live tomorrow.

So let this chapter be your turning point. Make the choice to renew your mind daily. Speak God's promises over your life. Think intentionally, live intentionally. Because once you win the battle in your mind, you will start to see victory in every area such as your relationships, your work, your habits, and even your health.

With God on your side, your mind doesn't have to be a place of confusion, fear, or defeat. It can be a place of peace, clarity, and power. And that, my friend, is where true transformation begins.

Understanding Your Thought Patterns

Every day, thousands of thoughts run through our minds, some helpful, others harmful. Many of these thoughts come and go so quickly that we don't even notice them. But over time, the patterns they form begin to shape our emotions, decisions, and actions. That's why it's important to slow down and understand what's really going on in your mind.

Do you often catch yourself thinking, "*I'm not good enough,*" "*Things never work out for me,*" or "*What if something goes wrong?*" These kinds of thoughts, when repeated over and over, can become mental habits. And just like any habit, they can be changed but only if you first become aware of them.

Your thought patterns can either lift you up or weigh you down. If your mind constantly leans toward fear, doubt, or negativity, it will quietly hold you back from living the life God created for you. But when you begin to shift your focus—choosing to think about what is true, hopeful, and full of God's promises—your mindset, and eventually your life, will begin to change.

"Whatever is true, whatever is noble, whatever is right, whatever is pure, whatever is lovely, whatever is admirable—if anything is excellent or praiseworthy—think about such things." - **Philippians 4:8**

This is not just positive thinking—it's biblical

thinking. It's training your mind to agree with God's truth, even when your feelings or the world say otherwise.

Changing your thought patterns doesn't happen overnight, but it *does* happen with practice. Each time you choose truth over lies, hope over fear, and faith over doubt, you're building a stronger, healthier mind. So, take the first step. Start listening to your thoughts. Challenge the ones that don't line up with God's Word. And little by little, you'll find yourself thinking, living, and walking in the freedom and purpose He has always planned for you.

Replacing Lies with God's Truth

Many people struggle with negative or limiting thoughts, not because they enjoy them, but because they don't recognize them as lies. Over time, these thoughts feel normal. "I'm not good enough." "Nothing ever works out for me." "God blesses others, not people like me." These are not only harmful thoughts but they are lies that keep you stuck, discouraged, and far from the life God wants for you.

But here's the good news: You don't have to stay trapped in these lies. The Bible teaches that in Christ, you are deeply loved, fully forgiven, chosen, and blessed. Ephesians 1:3-6 reminds us that we have every spiritual blessing in Christ and that God chose us in love before the foundation of the world. The problem is, many believers *know* this in theory but don't *believe* it in their hearts. That's where true transformation begins by replacing old beliefs with the truths.

As **Kenneth E. Hagin** rightly said in his book ***Knowing What Belongs to Us***, *"We must know what belongs to us in the redemption through Christ Jesus.* In one session of **'Rise of the Prophetic Voice'**, ***Minister Waza*** and ***Minister Hazzel***, both lawyers, explained that from a legal perspective, you must know what belongs to you in a contract before you can claim it. If you don't know your rights and blessings as a child of God, you may end up living far below your potential, thinking you're just "getting by," when God has already given you everything you need.

There's a well-known story that perfectly illustrates this point.

A poor father once sent his son overseas to study. After graduating and settling down, the son sent his father a premium ship ticket so they could finally live together. When the father boarded the ship, he didn't realize what the ticket included. He brought simple food from home, slept on the floor, and even did odd jobs to earn meals on the ship.

When he arrived, he told his son, "The journey was fine, but I ran out of food and had to work for it." The son was shocked. "Father, your ticket was for *premium class*! All meals, a comfortable bed, and everything you needed was already included. You didn't have to struggle; you only had to *ask* and show your ticket!"

Many of us are like that father. We live in fear, stress, or spiritual lack—not because God hasn't provided, but because we don't realize what He's already given us through Christ. We keep striving, worrying, or settling for less, when God has already issued us a "premium ticket" through Jesus.

The key is this: Replace every lie with God's truth. But to do that, you must know the truth. And the truth is found in the Word of God.

Here's a **practical step** you can take starting today:

Pick one promise from God's Word each week. Write it down, memorize it, speak it aloud every day, and whenever a lie comes up, *answer it* with that truth. For Example -

Lie: "I'm not good enough." → Truth: "I am God's masterpiece, created for good works." (Ephesians 2:10)

Lie: "I'm always alone." → Truth: "God will never leave me or forsake me." (Hebrews 13:5)

The more you repeat God's truth, the more it will replace the lies in your heart. Just like a dirty glass gets clean as you keep pouring fresh water into it, your mind will be renewed as you keep pouring in the truth of God's Word.

Remember: **You don't need to earn God's promises; they've already been given.** But you do need to *receive them*, *believe them*, and *walk in them*. When you replace the lies with His truth, you'll begin to live with the confidence, joy, and peace that come from knowing who you really are in Christ.

Developing a Winner's Mindset

"Faith without attitude is an empty shell, like a car without an engine." – ***Apostle Dr. Alph Lukau***

You must develop a winner's mindset and attitude. From a biblical point of view, this means learning to see yourself and your future through what the Bible says, trusting God's promises more than your current problems, emotions, or the opinions of others.

The Bible is full of powerful promises. It says you are more than a conqueror ***(Romans 8:37)***, that all things are possible for those who believe ***(Mark 9:23)***, and that God has good plans for your life ***(Jeremiah 29:11)***. When life gets hard or things don't go your way, don't let those situations shape your thinking. Instead, remind yourself what God says about you. Think of David, He faced huge challenges, including giants and entire armies. Yet, he always spoke with confidence and faith. He trusted in God's power, not in the size of the problem.

In God's kingdom, winners are not just people who hope for better things. They are people who trust deeply in what Jesus has already done for them.

"Do not throw away your confidence; it will be richly rewarded." - ***Hebrews 10:35***

This kind of confidence doesn't come from your background, skills, or feelings. It comes from knowing your identity in Christ and trusting the victory He has already given you. It means you don't just wish that something will work out, rather you believe it will, because God is working behind the scenes, even if you can't see it yet.

Imagine a runner who already knows he will win the race. He runs with boldness and peace, not fear. In the same way, when you believe in God's promises, you can face life's battles with calm assurance, not just wishful thinking.

However, no matter how much you pray or dream, you won't experience real victory if your thinking stays negative. Proverbs 23:7 says, "As a man thinks in his heart, so is he." If you are always telling yourself things like, "I'm a failure," or "I'll never change," then you're blocking your own growth—even if God's Word says you're victorious. My spiritual father **Apostle Dr. Alph Lukau** says, *"You cannot have right if your thinking is wrong."* God wants to transform your thinking, because your thoughts shape your life.

Think about the Israelites who were afraid to enter the Promised Land. In **Numbers 13:33**, they said, *"We seemed like grasshoppers in our own eyes."* They didn't believe what God had already promised, so they missed out. In the same way, if you keep seeing yourself as weak or unworthy, you might miss the blessings that are already yours.

God wants you to see yourself the way He sees you—loved, chosen, and fully equipped to win. With a mindset grounded in His truth, you can live with confidence, joy, and strength no matter what challenges come your way.

Practical Steps to Change Your Thinking

Changing the way you think does not happen in one day. But with daily effort and trust in God's Word, your thoughts can be transformed. Here are simple and practical steps you can take to begin renewing your mind:

1. Identify Negative Thoughts

Start by becoming aware of the thoughts that regularly go through your mind, especially those that are negative, limiting, or filled with fear. You may often think things like, "I can't do this," or "Nothing ever works for me." Write down these thoughts so you can recognize the patterns.

2. Keep a Thought Journal

Take a few minutes each day to write down what you are thinking—especially during moments when you feel anxious, angry, or sad. Over time, you will begin to notice repeated fears or lies you have been believing. Becoming aware is the first step to breaking free.

3. Practice the Pause and Reflect Method

When a negative or discouraging thought enters your mind, pause and ask yourself: "Is this really true?" and "What does God's Word say about this?" Replace that thought with truth. For example, if you think, "I am not good enough," remind yourself: "I am fearfully and wonderfully made" **(Psalm 139:14).**

4. Set Daily Reminders of Truth

Write encouraging Bible verses or declarations on sticky notes and place them where you will see them often—like your mirror, desk, fridge, or phone screen. These reminders help keep your focus on what is good and true.

5. Meditate on Scripture Daily

Spend time each day reading and thinking deeply about a verse from the Bible. Choose one that speaks to your current situation and repeat it to yourself throughout the day. Do not just read it—think about what it means for your life and how you can live it out.

6. Speak Life-Giving Words

What you say affects what you think. Begin speaking positive and faith-filled words based on God's promises. Say things like, "God is working in my life," or "I am loved and accepted by God." The more you speak the truth, the more your mind will begin to believe it.

7. Practice Thankfulness Every Day

Start your day by thanking God for specific blessings, no matter how small they seem. Gratitude shifts your focus away from problems and helps you see the good things in your life. Try writing down three things you are thankful for each day.

8. Surround Yourself with Positive Influences

Spend time with people who encourage your faith and speak hope into your life. Listen to uplifting music, read inspiring books, and avoid content that fills your mind with fear or comparison. Unfollow or unsubscribe from people or pages that make you feel low or unworthy.

9. Ask God for Help in Prayer

Ask the Holy Spirit to help you notice and reject negative thoughts. Pray for a peaceful and focused mind. **James 1:5** reminds us, *"If any of you lacks wisdom, ask God, who gives freely to all without finding fault."*

10. Take Every Thought Captive

When a wrong thought comes, do not let it stay. Challenge it right away. **2 Corinthians 10:5** says, *"We take every thought captive to make it obedient to Christ."* Picture yourself grabbing the thought and replacing it with God's truth.

By practicing these steps each day, you will start to see real change in your thinking. Your thoughts will align more with God's truth, and that will reflect in your actions and your life. Remember, this is a journey, and God is walking with you every step of the way.

Guarding Your Mind

Guarding your mind means protecting what you allow into your thoughts, emotions, and beliefs. Why is this important? Because your mind shapes the way you live and the choices you make.

"Keep your heart with all diligence, for out of it spring the issues of life." - ***Proverbs 4:23***

In the Bible, the "heart" often refers to your inner thoughts and emotions—what we now call the mind.

Just like a gate control what enters a city, you need to control what enters your mind. Whatever you read, watch, or listen to will affect how you think, feel, and act. If you allow negative or harmful content in—like gossip, lies, or fear—it can slowly pull you away from God's truth.

Think of it like your diet. You wouldn't eat spoiled food because it harms your body. In the same way, don't feed your mind with unhealthy things, be intentional. Spend time with people who speak life and hope, and avoid those who bring constant negativity or distraction. Choose carefully what you allow in, because your thoughts shape your actions and your future.

To guard your mind well, start by filling it with God's truth.

"Let the word of Christ dwell in you richly." -

Colossians 3:16

This means making Scripture a regular part of your life. When your mind is full of God's Word, you can more easily recognize lies and reject them.

Philippians 4:8 teaches us to focus on things that are "true, noble, right, pure, lovely, and admirable." This means choosing to think about what is good and uplifting rather than focusing on fear, anger, or negativity.

Also, **Philippians 4:6–7** tells us that when we pray and trust God, His peace will guard our hearts and minds. So, when you're feeling anxious or overwhelmed, take time to pray and trust that God is in control.

Guarding your mind takes daily effort, but with God's help, you can protect your thoughts and live in peace and purpose. A healthy mind leads to a transformed life.

Walking in the New Mindset

Adopting a new mindset in Christ doesn't happen overnight. It's a process that takes time, effort, and patience. When you begin to think according to God's truth instead of old habits or negative thoughts, you're taking an important step toward the purpose God has for your life.

There may be times when you struggle or slip back into old thinking patterns. That's okay. Don't feel discouraged. A new mindset is something you grow into, one day at a time. It's about moving forward, not being perfect. Every time you choose to believe what God says about you instead of what fear or doubt says, you grow stronger.

You're not doing this alone. The Holy Spirit is always with you, ready to help, guide, and strengthen your mind when you ask. Like someone training for a marathon, your mind needs daily training—through reading the Bible, praying, and choosing to think positively and truthfully.

In the beginning, it might feel hard or even frustrating. But if you keep going, change will come. Over time, you'll notice the negative thoughts losing their power and God's peace taking their place. You'll think more clearly, act more confidently, and feel more joyful.

Keep moving forward. Speak God's promises over yourself. Invite the Holy Spirit to shape your thoughts. And don't forget to celebrate your small wins. Each step brings you closer to living the life God designed for you—one filled with purpose, hope, and victory.

Chapter 3

Clarifying Goals: Setting God-Aligned Intentions

What Is a Goal?

A goal is simply a destination—something you decide to move toward. It could be as ordinary as buying groceries or as life-changing as finding your purpose in life. For example, if your goal is to buy groceries, you first decide what you need. Then you break that goal into smaller steps like leaving the house, getting into the car, driving to the store, and picking up the items. Along the way, you might face challenges like bad weather or low fuel. But you find solutions, like taking an umbrella or stopping at a fuel station. Once you finish shopping and return home, you feel a sense of success and move on to the next task.

This is how goals work. You set a clear outcome, plan the steps, face and solve problems, and keep going until the goal is reached. Then you celebrate the win, no matter how small it seems. This same pattern applies to bigger goals too. Whether it is about career, relationships, health, or spiritual growth—the process of setting a goal, making a plan, taking action, and staying committed remains the same.

Unlike daydreams or random wishes, a goal is clear and specific. It is not just hoping for something good to happen someday. It requires focus, effort, and action. Wishes can fade, but goals guide your decisions. Without a goal, life can feel directionless. But when you have a goal, you move with purpose. You know where you are going and what steps you need to take to get there.

From the time of Adam till today, the idea of setting goals has not changed. People have always aimed for something, made plans, faced difficulties, and adjusted their approach until they achieved what they wanted. The tools and strategies may look different now, but the human drive to set and reach goals has remained the same throughout history.

Life is full of desires and dreams. Some are small and pass quickly, while others are deep and long-term. Some goals take only a few minutes to complete, while others require months or even years of effort. In this chapter, we will focus on the kind of goals that have the power to transform your life and the lives of others around you—goals that align with a greater purpose and give your journey true meaning. You will also learn how to set such goals in a practical way and work steadily towards achieving them.

The Importance of Setting Goals

"So when Jesus had received the sour wine, He said, 'It is finished!' And bowing His head, He gave up His spirit." - ***John 19:30***

When Jesus died on the cross and said, "*It is finished*", He was not speaking as someone who had wandered through life without direction. These were the words of a man who had completed His mission. What was finished? The work of redemption was complete, The debt of sin had been paid in full, The requirements of the Old Covenant were fulfilled, The path to reconciliation with God was now open, Victory over sin, death, and the devil was accomplished. Jesus had fulfilled the purpose for which He came to earth.

"He who sins is of the devil, for the devil has sinned from the beginning. For this purpose the Son of God was manifested, that He might destroy the works of the devil." - ***1 John 3:8***

The Bible tells us clearly, '*For this purpose Jesus came...*' Jesus didn't just come to forgive sins, but to break the power of sin, sickness, fear, bondage, and every dark force. His life was not filled with random actions. Every step, every miracle, every decision was part of a divine plan laid out before time began.

Jesus even fulfilled specific prophecies down to the smallest detail. He was born in Bethlehem, just as the Scriptures foretold **(Matthew 2:5–6)**. He lived in Nazareth so that He would be called a Nazarene (Matthew 2:23). His triumphal entry into Jerusalem also fulfilled prophecy (Matthew 21). None of these events happened by chance; each one was part of a heavenly plan being carried out on earth. My spiritual father, **Apostle Dr Alph Lukau**, often says, *"There is nothing random in the Kingdom of God."* And this is true not only for Jesus but also for us.

If even a regular church service requires planning, how much more should our lives be guided by purpose? Think about it: if a worship leader starts singing a song the choir does not know, the musicians play in a different key, and the preacher goes on too long, everything becomes confusing. It creates disorder. That is why even the smallest service must be planned and structured.

Now consider your own life. Is it not more important than a one-hour meeting? Your calling, your purpose, your future—all deserve thoughtful preparation. Just moving fast is not enough. As my spiritual father says, *"Speed in the wrong direction would lead you to the wrong destination..."* It is not just about movement; it is about direction. Without clear goals, you may work hard but end up far from where you are meant to be.

Let's say you want to travel from Dubai to America.

You don't just get excited and go to the airport. You must decide which city you are going to, which airline to book, whether it's a direct or connecting flight, how long it will take, and what to carry. You even plan your arrival like which hotel you will stay in. Without this level of planning, you risk delays, confusion, or even ending up in the wrong place.

In the same way, setting clear goals in life is not optional, rather it is essential. Whether you are a student, a businessperson, an employee, or serving in ministry, you need defined goals to guide you. When you set goals, you focus your energy. You make better decisions. You prepare for challenges and find solutions. You measure your progress and celebrate your growth. Most importantly, you align your life with God's greater purpose.

God's work is always marked by planning, order, and completion. He says in **Jeremiah 29:11**, *"For I know the plans I have for you,"* showing us that our lives are not random but part of a well-thought-out design. Setting goals aligned with God's will is more than just good discipline—it is an act of faith. It shows that you believe your life has meaning and that you are a steward of the time, talents, and opportunities God has given you.

A life with clear, God-centered goals will not feel limited, it will feel focused and full of purpose. Instead of being pulled in every direction, you will walk with clarity, direction, and confidence, just like Jesus did. Setting goals is not about controlling every detail of your future, it is about walking in partnership with God's plan, one step at a time.

God's Will and Your Goals

It is God's will that you prosper in every area of your life. Whether you are preparing for an exam, starting a business, aiming for a promotion, or trying to live a healthier lifestyle, God wants you to succeed. This is not just a hopeful idea; it is rooted in the Word of God. God takes delight in your progress and growth. The Bible says,

"Beloved, I pray that you may prosper in all things and be in health, just as your soul prospers" - ***3 John 1:2***

Psalm 1:3 says, *"He shall be like a tree planted by the rivers of water... and whatever he does shall prosper."* This verse paints a picture of stability, nourishment, and steady growth. Just as a tree planted near water flourishes, God desires that you grow strong and bear fruit in every season of life.

However, God's idea of success is not just about achieving personal dreams or gaining more things. Real success comes when your goals are aligned with God's will and bring benefit to others, not harm. The Bible gives clear guidance about this. **Proverbs 16:3** says, *"Commit your works to the Lord, and your thoughts will be established."* In **Proverbs 16:9**, it says, *"A man's heart plans his way, but the Lord directs his steps."* And

James 4:13–15 reminds us that while we may make plans, only God knows what will truly happen. This means that our planning must come with humility, and we must seek God's guidance at every step.

Not every goal is a godly goal. Some ambitions may seem profitable but actually go against God's principles. For example, a business that sells harmful products like cigarettes might bring financial gain, but it destroys lives. Such goals can never carry God's blessing. As one preacher said, *"You can fight God and win, but that's the worst kind of victory."* Jesus Himself asked, "*What will it profit a man if he gains the whole world, and loses his own soul?"* **(Mark 8:36).**

The key is to invite God into your goal-setting process from the very beginning. **Proverbs 3:5–6** teaches, *"In all your ways acknowledge Him, and He shall direct your paths."* When you acknowledge God and surrender your plans to Him, He will guide your steps. This is not just a spiritual idea but a very practical one. The Holy Spirit can show you whether to go forward, wait, or take a different route. As **Isaiah 30:21** promises, *"Your ears shall hear a word behind you, saying, 'This is the way, walk in it,' whenever you turn to the right hand or whenever you turn to the left."*

Sometimes God will confirm your direction with peace. Other times, He may gently stop you or shift your path. This is how we walk in partnership with Him—not just making plans and asking Him to bless them, but allowing Him to lead from the start.

Your dreams matter to God. Aligning them with His will does not make them smaller, rather it makes them stronger. Goals that come from God bless others, not just yourself. They bring peace, not pressure. They bring fulfilment, not regret. When your goals are shaped by God's heart, you move forward with confidence, knowing you are walking in His purpose for your life.

Biblical Principles for Goal-Setting

When setting goals as believers, the first and most important step is to make sure they honor God. Biblical goals are not driven by selfish ambition or personal pride. Instead, they are rooted in love, purpose, and a desire to reflect the values of God's Kingdom. Jesus said,

"Seek first the Kingdom of God and His righteousness, and all these things shall be added to you" ***- Matthew 6:33.***

This means that our goals should reflect His character, bring Him glory, and advance His work on earth.

Godly goals also bless others. They build people up, serve communities, and come from a heart that wants to make a positive difference. As the Bible teaches in **Romans 12:10–13**, we are called to love sincerely, serve with zeal, and meet the needs of those around us. In short, true biblical goals honor God, bless others, and reflect values like justice, mercy, humility, and faith.

Along with clear purpose, biblical goal-setting also involves faith, humility, and dependence on God. Faith means trusting that God can open doors and lead us even when we cannot see the full picture. Humility means holding our plans loosely, always ready to say,

"If the Lord wills, we will live and do this or that" - ***James 4:15*** **.**

Dependence on God means seeking Him through prayer, listening for His guidance, and submitting our plans to Him at every stage. As **Proverbs 16:3** reminds us, *"Commit your works to the Lord, and your thoughts will be established."*

The Bible gives us many powerful examples of godly goal-setters. **Nehemiah** saw the broken walls of Jerusalem and turned to prayer before taking action. He planned wisely, led boldly, and kept seeking God as he rebuilt the city. **Paul** had a clear goal—to preach the gospel where Christ was not yet known. He planned his journeys carefully but remained sensitive to the Spirit's leading, even when plans changed. **Jesus**, the perfect example, lived with full awareness of His mission. Every step of His life fulfilled prophecy, and He always surrendered His will to the Father, saying, *"Not My will, but Yours be done"* **(Luke 22:42).**

In the end, setting goals the biblical way is not just about achieving something. It is about walking with God, growing in character, and allowing Him to shape your path. When your goals are aligned with His will, your life gains direction, strength, and purpose—both in the journey and in the result.

How to Set Goals

Turning Intentions into Action

A goal without a plan is only a wish. Once you have set your goal, the next step is to make it real by creating a clear and practical action plan. A dream remains vague unless you know exactly how to achieve it. Planning turns your goals into a pathway you can follow every day.

The best way to approach any big goal is to break it into smaller and more manageable parts. For example, if you have a one-year goal, start by dividing it into quarterly milestones. Then, break each quarter into monthly targets, and finally into daily tasks. This makes even the largest goal feel achievable.

Let's say your goal is to pass an important exam within a year. Begin by dividing the subjects and study materials into four sections, one for each quarter of the year. Each quarter is then broken down into monthly portions, such as covering a few chapters from each subject. If you have 12 chapters across three subjects to read in a month (in 25 Days, we'll learn about '*buffer*' later), you can aim to finish one chapter every two days. This transforms an overwhelming challenge into a clear, daily achievable task.

Daily diligence is the key. The Bible reminds us,

"Let us not become weary in doing good, for at the proper time we will reap a harvest if we do not give up" - ***Galatians 6:9***

Discipline and consistent effort are what separate achievement from wishful thinking. Some days will be more difficult than others, but steady, faithful work builds up over time and leads to success.

Turning intentions into action means having a plan, breaking down your goal into daily steps, staying accountable, and regularly reviewing your progress (We'll cover in later chapters). When you persevere and stay committed, dreams slowly transform into reality.

Setting Balanced Goals

When you set goals, it is important to divide them into the key areas of your life. This helps you build a balanced approach that reflects the full journey God has planned for you. Many people focus only on one area, such as career, money, or personal success, but God desires to bless and guide every part of your life.

Consider including sections such as faith, family, health, career, relationships, finances, service, and personal growth. Giving attention to each of these areas makes your goal-setting more complete and aligned with how God cares for your whole life, not just one part.

This balanced approach helps you stay focused without becoming one-sided. It allows you to notice new opportunities and remain open to God's presence in every part of your journey. As you pray and work toward your goals, it reminds you that growth is not only about worldly success but also about becoming the person God created you to be.

The Bible says, "Jesus increased in wisdom and stature, and in favor with God and man" (Luke 2:52). This verse shows that even Jesus grew in a balanced way—spiritually, mentally, physically, and socially. In the same way, your goals should reflect balance, growth, and blessing in every area of life.

1. Faith and Ministry Goals

"But seek first the kingdom of God and His righteousness, and all these things shall be added to you" - ***Matthew 6:33***

One of the most important areas of your goals-setting should be faith and ministry. This is where you set goals that will help you grow closer to God and serve Him more faithfully. For example, you may commit to reading the entire Bible by the end of the year, or you might set a goal to strengthen your prayer life such as praying for one hour each day or at least five days a week. You could also include fasting once a week to deepen your spiritual walk and seek God's guidance.

If you are in ministry, your goals-setting can include goals for evangelism, such as reaching out to a certain number of people each month with the gospel, or discipleship goals, like mentoring a few individuals in their faith journey. These goals keep your focus on serving others while also strengthening your relationship with God. When your vision begins with God's Kingdom, every other part of life falls into place. Your faith and ministry goals will not only guide your spiritual growth but will also align the rest of your vision with God's will.

2. Family and Relationship Goals

Your goals-setting should also include goals for family and relationships, because these are gifts from God that need love and care. If you are married, set goals to strengthen your bond with your spouse, such as going on regular outings, spending quality time together, or simply creating moments of appreciation and support. If you have children, include goals that help you be present in their lives like joining them in their hobbies, helping with studies, or engaging in fun activities that build trust and memories.

Friendships and community bonds are also important. You can set goals to stay connected with friends, check in regularly, or serve together in meaningful ways. Being intentional about these relationships strengthens not only your personal life but also the community around you.

"Above all, love each other deeply..." **- 1 Peter 4:8**

Building strong family and relationship goals ensures that love remains at the center, creating unity, joy, and lasting bonds that honor God.

3. Career and Business Goals

Your goals-setting should also include goals for your career, studies, or business. God has given each of us talents and abilities, and it is our responsibility to develop them faithfully. If you are a student, you can set goals for completing certification courses, preparing for competitive exams, or improving your skills in areas that will shape your future. If you are working, you might include goals for learning new skills, taking leadership training, or finding ways to grow in your profession.

For those who run a business, set goals to expand your knowledge in entrepreneurship, improve leadership skills, or take courses that help you manage and grow your company effectively. And if you are called to ministry, you can include goals like attending speaking classes, learning better ways to manage your ministry, or developing skills to serve people more fruitfully.

"Whatever you do, work at it with all your heart, as working for the Lord, not for human masters" -

Colossians 3:23

When you see your career or business as a way to honor God, your goals become not just about success but about serving with excellence and glorifying Him through your work.

4. Health and Wellness Goals

The Bible teaches us that our body is the temple of the Holy Spirit, and caring for it is both a responsibility and an act of worship. Health and wellness are not just about looking good but about honoring God with the strength and energy He has given us. Setting goals in this area helps us build habits that support a long, fruitful, and joyful life.

You can include goals like regular exercise to keep your body active and strong, eating healthy foods that nourish you, and drinking enough water each day. Just as important is caring for your mental and emotional health. You may set goals to rest well, take breaks when needed, read uplifting books, spend time in nature, or practice gratitude daily. These small but consistent habits can protect you from stress and burnout.

"Do you not know that your bodies are temples of the Holy Spirit, who is in you, whom you have received from God? You are not your own" ***- 1 Corinthians 6:19***

Remember that true wellness is balance. It means strengthening your body, refreshing your mind, and keeping your spirit alive in God's presence. When you take care of your health, you are also caring for the temple where God's Spirit lives.

5. Finances and Stewardship Goals

God has already blessed us with every spiritual blessing in Christ, and He desires that we also walk in wisdom concerning our financial life. To experience the fullness of what He has given, we must set clear and intentional goals. You cannot reach a target that you do not see, so having financial goals gives you direction and discipline.

"The borrower is slave to the lender" - ***Proverbs 22:7***

One important goal is to live free from the bondage of debt. Debt steals peace and limits opportunities, so you should make plans to pay it off and refuse to let it control your future. Along with this, set goals to save and invest wisely. I have published a book on personal finance titled ***'The Richest in Modern Times'***. It is written in the Indian context; however, the principles of finance apply universally in any part of the world. Even small, consistent steps in saving prepare you for future needs and open doors for growth.

"Remember the Lord your God, for it is He who gives you the ability to produce wealth" - ***Deuteronomy 8:18***

Equally important is generosity. God blesses us so that we can also be a blessing to others. You can create goals for giving or acts of kindness like committing one or two students' school fees or helping an orphanage every month. In our ministry we have an '**AL Partners**' program which reaches out to the needy. When you give with a cheerful heart, you align with God's promise of abundance.

With discipline, wisdom, and a heart of gratitude, your financial goals can become a testimony of God's faithfulness.

6. Personal Growth Goals

In a world that is constantly changing, personal growth is not optional but necessary. To thrive, you must set goals that help you adapt, learn, and stay relevant. This can include learning new technologies, exploring useful software, or developing new skills like use of AI that make you more effective in your work and life. Growth is not only about professional development but also about becoming the best version of yourself.

Personal growth also includes goals that bring joy and balance to life. You can set goals for hobbies that refresh your mind, such as music, painting, or reading. Travel can also be a goal, as it opens your eyes to new cultures, experiences, and perspectives. Creativity in any form allows you to express the gifts God has placed in you.

"Let the wise listen and add to their learning, and let the discerning get guidance" - ***Proverbs 1:5***

Growth is a lifelong journey, and every new skill or experience makes you more prepared for the opportunities God places before you. By setting personal growth goals, you invest in yourself and stay ready for the future while enjoying the present.

7. **Service and Ministry Goals**

A complete vision for life should also include the desire to serve others. God has called every believer not only to live for themselves but also to bless the world around them. Service can take many forms like volunteering in your community, supporting your church, or using your gifts to encourage and uplift people.

If God has given you talents like music, you can create Gospel songs that inspire faith. If you enjoy writing, you can share words of encouragement on social media to strengthen the weary and give hope to the oppressed. Even small acts of service, like helping a neighbour or mentoring someone younger in faith, are powerful ways to reflect Christ's love.

"Each of you should use whatever gift you have received to serve others, as faithful stewards of God's grace in its various forms" - **1 Peter 4:10**

Service is not just about what you do but about the heart with which you do it. When you set goals for ministry and service, you are aligning your vision with God's greater purpose—becoming His salt and light in the world.

Making Your Goals Measurable

Once you have set goals for each area of your life, the next step is to make them measurable. Remember, less is more. It is better to focus on a few clear and realistic goals than to set too many and feel overwhelmed. This will keep you motivated and help you make steady progress. As the saying goes, "*What is measurable is manageable.*" When you measure your goals, you can track your progress, make adjustments where needed, and celebrate milestones along the way. Once **Dad Alph** said, *"Changing your ways is always a sign of maximizing opportunity."* Without measuring your progress, you leave no room to correct or adjust your efforts to make the most of them.

Writing goals clearly and making them measurable gives clarity and direction to our lives.

Types of Measurable Goals

1. Duration or Unit Goals – These are goals measured by time or units. For example, "I will exercise for 45 minutes each day," "I will save $500 this month," or "I will read 10 pages of the Bible daily." This type of goal is easy to track because it has a clear quantity or duration attached to it.

2. Countable Goals – These are goals you can count by numbers. For example, "I will take 10,000 steps daily," "I will share the Gospel with 5 people this week," or "I will write 3 chapters of my book this month." Countable goals make it simple to know whether or not you are reaching your targets.

3. Yes or No Goals – Some goals are not measured by numbers but by action itself. For example, "Did I wake up at 5 a.m.?" or "Did I pray for one hour today?" These goals are straightforward—either you did them or you did not. Even though they are simple, they are powerful in building consistency and discipline.

Be Specific and Realistic

Some goals are based on outcomes, such as "lose 30 pounds in a year," while others focus on actions, such as "exercise 45 minutes a day." Both are valuable, depending on what motivates you. The key is to be specific and realistic. For example, saying "I want to earn more money" is vague, but setting a target like "I will earn $1,000 extra this month" makes it measurable and achievable. Here, being realistic does not mean doubting God's ability to perform miracles with no reference. It means being realistic about our efforts while still leaving room for the miracle-working God.

Set Deadlines

Every goal needs a time frame. If your goal is to save $50,000, ask yourself '*by when?*' Deadlines give you accountability and urgency. Some goals may be short-term (6 months), others medium-term (1 year), and some long-term (5 years).

There are also recurring goals, like reading the Bible daily or exercising every day. These do not have an endpoint, but you can still track your consistency to see your progress.

Organize and Track

To stay on course, divide your goals into categories. Some will be **measurable in numbers, some countable by actions,** and some will be simple '**yes-or-no'** commitments. Once categorized, set achievable deadlines for the ones that require a clear target. For recurring habits, focus on building consistency rather than a finish line.

By writing, measuring, and tracking your goals, you give structure to your goals. This not only makes them achievable but also strengthens your faith, because every small step of progress is a testimony of God's grace working in your life.

The Power of Chunking

Chunking means breaking a big task or goal into small, manageable pieces. It is a simple strategy, but it is incredibly powerful for turning dreams into real results. As we have set both short-term and long-term goals on our goals-setting. The next step is to "***chunk***" these larger goals into daily or weekly action steps that feel achievable instead of overwhelming.

When you break large goals into small steps, they stop being intimidating. Instead of worrying about the entire journey, you only focus on what needs to be done today or this week. Progress begins to build naturally, and with every small step completed, you move closer to your vision.

Example 1: Reading Goals, Suppose you want to read 10 books this year to improve your career skills. At first, this can feel like a big task. But chunking makes it simple. Instead of thinking about 10 books, you divide the goal into monthly or daily targets. 10 books a year means 1 book per month (with 2 months left as a buffer). If each book is about 250 pages, then reading 10 pages per day will allow you to finish one book each month. This way, your yearly goal of 10 books becomes very realistic and easy to achieve.

Example 2: Financial Goals, Let's say you aim to save $25,000 in one year. Instead of looking at the whole number and feeling overwhelmed, chunk it into smaller goals. $25,000 per year equals about $2,100 each month. Now, your focus becomes saving $2,000 each month, which feels much more achievable. By sticking to this smaller monthly goal, you will naturally accomplish the bigger yearly target.

When you chunk down every medium or long-term goal into daily or weekly tasks, the overwhelming vision suddenly feels possible. Instead of being discouraged by a huge dream, you simply do what is required today. This not only reduces anxiety but also builds confidence and momentum. Each small achievement strengthens your faith and keeps you moving forward. Faithfulness in the small steps prepares you for greater victories ahead. Chunking helps you stay motivated, organized, and faithful to your journey—making every step count!

Common Mistakes in Goal-Setting

One of the most common mistakes in goal-setting is creating unrealistic goals. Sometimes, in our excitement, we take Bible verses like "*nothing is impossible with God*" ***(Luke 1:37)*** out of context. We forget that faith must work hand in hand with wisdom, planning, and hard work.

For example, in a time of famine, God miraculously fed Elijah through ravens **(1 Kings 17:6)**. Yet Paul, serving the same God, still worked as a tentmaker to support himself ***(Acts 18:3)***. He even taught, "*If anyone will not work, neither shall he eat*" ***(2 Thessalonians 3:10)***. Faith is not an excuse for laziness or wishful thinking. You cannot be earning $4,000 a month and set a goal to earn $40,000 in six months without a clear and realistic plan. Such expectations set us up for disappointment and can weaken our motivation. God calls us to trust Him, but also to plan wisely, work diligently, and steward resources well.

Another mistake is assuming everything will go exactly as planned. Some think that if God opens a door, the path will be smooth. But Scripture shows us that open doors often come with challenges. Paul said,

> *"For a great and effective door has opened to me, and there are many adversaries"* ***- 1 Corinthians 16:9***

He also shared that "*Satan hindered us*" ***(1***

Thessalonians 2:18). Even Jesus said, "*In the world you will have tribulation; but be of good cheer, I have overcome the world*" ***(John 16:33)***. We must prepare for delays, obstacles, and unexpected turns, trusting God's guidance through them all.

We also underestimate the inner battles that can stop our progress. Procrastination, fear, distractions, discouragement, and failure can all weaken our focus. There will be days when things do not go as planned. Even while writing this book, I have faced setbacks and challenges. But these do not define me, because I know, "*We are more than conquerors through Him who loved us*" ***(Romans 8:37)***. We fight from a place of victory, not for victory.

The truth is, setbacks and resistance are part of the journey. They are not signs to give up, but opportunities to grow stronger. A mature, faith-filled approach to goal-setting plans carefully, expects difficulties, stays rooted in Scripture, and presses forward with courage.

Deadlines and Timelines

"For though by this time you ought to be teachers, you need someone to teach you again the first principles of the oracles of God; and you have come to need milk and not solid food." — ***Hebrews 5:12***

Here, Paul is essentially pointing out that because of not following a clear deadline and an actionable plan, the believers had remained just like spiritual babies—stuck in the basics when they should have matured into teachers. The same principle applies to our personal and professional goals: without clear timelines, we remain in a cycle of *"starting over"* instead of progressing forward.

A very important step in reaching any goal is setting a clear deadline. A deadline turns your intention into a commitment. The moment you decide when you want to achieve something, it becomes real and urgent. Without a timeline, a goal remains a vague dream.

For bigger goals, it is wise to break them into smaller, measurable parts. If you have a ten-year vision, divide it into five-year, one-year, monthly, weekly, and even daily steps. This way you always know your next move. Progress comes from doing something every day, not just thinking about the far future.

Think about driving to a place that is 500 miles away. You cannot see the whole road ahead. In fact, you can only see about ten meters at a time. If you wait until you can see all 500 miles before starting, you will never leave. But if you drive forward the first ten meters, the next ten meters will appear. Step by step, you will travel the entire 500 miles. Goals work in the same way. You do not need to know exactly what will happen after five years. You just need to focus on what you have to do this week, and then the next step will appear.

Life is not always predictable. Sometimes you may miss your original deadline because of unexpected events, changes, or even miscalculations. This is normal.

The solution is not to give up, but to set a new deadline and keep moving forward. Most of the time, there are no impossible goals—only unrealistic timelines. Change your plan if needed, but keep your faith in the process.

Timelines are not just for big dreams; they work for daily life too. You can assign time slots to important activities. For example, you may choose two hours in the morning for study, the afternoon for practice, and the evening for prayer and reflection. This creates a healthy rhythm in your day and builds discipline.

Later, we will talk more about routines and time management. For now, remember this: consistency with deadlines—both long-term and daily—will keep you on track, give you motivation, and help you turn your goals into reality.

Chapter 4

Vision Boards

The Neuroscience of Vision Boards

Vision boards are powerful tools that combine creativity with purpose. When you create a vision board like choosing pictures, words, and scriptures that reflect your dreams, hopes, and faith, you are not just making something pretty to look at. You are engaging your brain in a way that can inspire real change.

Science shows that our brains respond strongly to images. When we see a picture that represents a goal, our brain processes it almost as if we are already experiencing it. This can stir up motivation, strengthen belief, and encourage us to take steps toward that goal. This is because of a God-given ability called **neuroplasticity**—our brain's capacity to adapt, grow, and form new connections throughout life.

What is Neuroplasticity?

Neuroplasticity simply means the brain's ability to learn and change. Every time we experience something new, practice a skill, or change a habit, our brain physically rewires itself to store that learning. You are not stuck with the brain you were born with—God has designed your brain to grow and reshape itself when you use it.

Our brain is made up of billions of nerve cells called ***neurons***, and they communicate with each other through connections called synapses. **Psalm 139:14** reminds us, "*We are fearfully and wonderfully made.*" When you repeat an action or a thought, the same group of neurons fire together. Over time, these connections grow stronger and faster. That is why people say, "Neurons that fire together, wire together." On the other hand, if you stop using a skill or a habit, those connections weaken, and it becomes harder to recall or perform.

Think of a child learning to ride a bicycle. At first, they wobble and struggle, but with practice, their brain builds new pathways that control balance, coordination, and timing. The same thing happens when you learn a new language, memorize a Bible verse, or break a harmful habit. With each repetition, your brain is literally changing its wiring.

Neuroplasticity works best when there is consistent practice and a stimulating environment. Just as muscles grow when you exercise them, your brain's wiring grows stronger when you challenge it with learning, problem-solving, and creativity. The beautiful truth is that this works at any age. Whether you are overcoming a fear, learning a new skill, or even recovering from an injury, your brain can adapt if you keep at it.

How Vision Boards Use Neuroplasticity

Vision boards work because they repeatedly expose your brain to the same images and words, reinforcing positive thinking and focus. Every time you look at your vision board, you activate memory, motivation, and planning centres in your brain. This repeated focus builds stronger connections between your thoughts and your actions, increasing your confidence to take steps toward your goals.

For believers, vision boards are more than just wish lists. They are a way to align your desires with God's will. When you create one, take time to pray and ask God for wisdom about what to include. Use scriptures that strengthen your faith and anchor your vision in His promises. **Proverbs 29:18** says, *"Where there is no vision, the people perish."* A vision board can help you keep God's vision for your life right in front of your eyes and heart.

In short, the neuroscience behind vision boards shows that what you repeatedly see and focus on shapes your thoughts, beliefs, and actions. And from a biblical perspective, when those thoughts are rooted in God's Word and guided by His Spirit, your vision board becomes more than a creative exercise—it becomes a faith-filled reminder that with God, all things are possible.

Abraham and Vision

The Bible gives us a deeper understanding of how God often uses visual aids to help His people grasp, believe, and remember His promises. One of the clearest examples of this is found in the life of Abraham, often called the father of faith.

God called Abraham to leave his homeland and follow Him into an unknown future, promising, *"I will make you a great nation"* **(Genesis 12:2)**. He told Abraham that he would be the father of many nations, even though at that time Abraham and Sarah had no children of their own.

This promise was not fulfilled immediately. Abraham had to wait many years before Isaac was born. During that long wait, it is not difficult to imagine the days when discouragement must have crept in—days when negative thoughts whispered that it was too late, that he and Sarah were now far too old for such a promise to come true. In the natural, everything about their situation seemed impossible.

Then God did something remarkable. Scripture says:

"Then He brought him outside and said, 'Look now toward heaven, and count the stars if you are able to number them.' And He said to him, 'So shall your offspring be'" - ***Genesis 15:5***

In that moment, the stars became more than just a beautiful night sky. They became a visual promise from God—a living picture that Abraham could see every single night. The stars were God's vision board for Abraham. Every time Abraham looked up, he had a physical, unchanging reminder of God's word to him. Even though he could not yet see the fulfillment in the natural, he could see it in the vision God placed before his eyes.

I sometimes imagine Abraham standing outside on a quiet night, looking up at the countless stars. On days when doubt tried to take over, when his mind reminded him of his age, he could lift his eyes and remember, "God promised me this." That sight kept hope alive. It was a God-given motivation tool that anchored him in the truth of God's faithfulness until the day the promise became reality.

In the same way, God often gives us prophetic words, dreams, and deep desires that align with His purposes for our lives. These may take time to come to pass. And in that waiting period, we may also face days of discouragement, moments when it feels like nothing is moving forward.

This is where a vision board becomes a powerful

tool for believers. Just as Abraham had the stars to look at, we can create our own faith-filled visual reminders of what God has spoken over our lives. When your vision board contains scriptures, prophetic words, and images that represent your calling, it becomes more than decoration—it becomes a daily anchor for your faith.

When you feel like giving up, one look at your vision board can spark inner motivation. It speaks to your heart just as the stars spoke to Abraham: ***Hold on. God who promised is faithful.***

"Let us hold fast the confession of our hope without wavering, for He who promised is faithful." -
Hebrews 10:23

Jacob and Vision

The story of Jacob in **Genesis 30** is one of the most fascinating examples in Scripture of how divine blessing can work hand in hand with human wisdom and creativity.

Jacob had been working for his uncle Laban for many years. Laban had deceived him several times, changing his wages again and again, yet Jacob continued to serve faithfully. Eventually, they came to a new agreement about Jacob's payment. Jacob said:

"...the speckled and spotted sheep, and all the brown ones among the lambs, and the spotted and speckled among the goats—these shall be my wages." **- Genesis 30:32**

Laban quickly agreed, but in his heart, he was already planning another trick. He removed all the speckled and spotted animals from the flock and gave them to his sons, sending them three days' journey away from Jacob **(Genesis 30:35)**. In doing this, Laban thought he had made it nearly impossible for Jacob to get any new spotted or speckled animals. Everyone knew that only if spotted and speckled animals mated could they produce more like them; if only plain-colored animals bred together, the offspring would also be plain. By removing all the spotted and speckled animals from the flock, Laban believed he had ensured that Jacob's share would remain small.

But Jacob was not naïve. He likely knew exactly what Laban was doing and may have even anticipated the trick. I imagine Jacob had grown up hearing family stories of faith—how God had shown Abraham the stars in the night sky as a visual promise of countless descendants. Perhaps Abraham had told this to Isaac, and Isaac had passed it on to Jacob, maybe as a treasured night-time story. Through these stories, Jacob may have learned that God often uses pictures and symbols to keep His promises alive in a person's heart. He understood the concept of a *"vision board"* long before we had a name for it, and he knew how to influence the outcome with what he had. So he let Laban do whatever he wanted, confident that God's wisdom would guide him to success. And so Jacob came up with a plan. Scripture says:

"Now Jacob took for himself rods of green poplar and of the almond and chestnut trees, peeled white strips in them, and exposed the white which was in the rods. And the rods which he had peeled, he set before the flocks in the gutters, in the watering troughs where the flocks came to drink, so that they should conceive when they came to drink. So the flocks conceived before the rods, and the flocks brought forth streaked, speckled, and spotted." - ***Genesis 30:37–39***

Jacob made a kind of vision board by taking rods from green poplar, almond, and chestnut trees, peeling white strips into them so they had streaks and spots, and placing them where the female sheep and goats would see them as they came to drink and breed. He was strategic, setting these patterned rods only before the stronger animals. As a result, the healthiest offspring carried the desired speckled and spotted markings, while the plain ones became fewer. This is a powerful illustration of how focused visual patterns—much like modern vision boards—can influence outcomes, and how, in our time, this principle connects with the concept of neuroplasticity.

To us today, this might seem mysterious. Science still cannot fully explain how the visual environment of animals could influence the markings of their young. But what we can see clearly is this: Jacob used the power of focused imagery to direct the outcome he was believing for.

From a neuroscience perspective, the brain's God-given ability to adapt and rewire itself when exposed repeatedly to certain images, thoughts, or experiences. For us, a vision board works the same way. When we continually focus on God-centered goals and promises, our minds begin to form patterns of thought, belief, and action that move us closer to them.

But the Bible also makes it very clear that this was not just Jacob's clever technique. Jacob later testified that it was God who had blessed him and given him success **(Genesis 31:9–12)**. The visual method was a tool, but the blessing came from the Lord.

In the same way, vision boards for us today are not magic and they are not a substitute for prayer. They are a way to keep God's promises in front of our eyes, to sharpen our faith, and to inspire us to take the steps we can. God's blessing and guidance remain the foundation but He also invites us to use wisdom, creativity, and the resources He has placed in our hands.

Note: *This teaching taught me by my friend* ***Apostle Sushil Macwan.***

How to make Vision boards

A Guide for Creating an Effective Faith-Driven Vision Board

1. Begin with Prayer and Reflection

"Your ears shall hear a word behind you, saying, 'This is the way, walk in it,' whenever you turn to the right hand or whenever you turn to the left." — ***Isaiah 30:21***

Begin by setting aside a quiet time to be in God's presence. Still your mind and heart so you can listen for His voice. Ask Him to reveal His will for your life, to shape your desires according to His plan, and to give you wisdom to know the difference between His direction and your own personal impulses.

Reflect deeply on your life's purpose, your hopes, and the dreams you believe He has placed within you. Think about the areas where you feel called to grow, the places where you need clarity, and the situations where you long for breakthrough. Writing these thoughts in a journal can help you see them clearly and keep track of how God is guiding you over time.

"Commit your works to the Lord, and your thoughts will be established." — ***Proverbs 16:3***

When you begin with prayer, you allow God to align your heart and mind with His Word. This makes the vision you create not just a reflection of your own wishes, but a partnership with Him in the plans He has for your life.

2. Gather Your Materials

Physical Vision Board - A physical vision board is something you can touch and interact with. The process of cutting, gluing, and arranging pictures engages your senses and makes your goals feel more real. You can decorate it with textures, keepsakes, or personal mementos that hold special meaning. Having it in your home or office serves as a constant visual anchor, reminding you of your vision every day. Building it can be a creative and reflective activity, and it works wonderfully for group or family projects where everyone contributes.

For a physical board, you will need a corkboard, poster board, or foam board, along with glue or pins, scissors, magazines, printed pictures, decorative items, and markers or stickers.

Digital Vision Board - A digital vision board can be updated instantly without starting over. It is easy to access anywhere through your phone or computer. You can include videos, worship music, or voice notes to make it even more inspiring. It can be shared with prayer groups or mentors for joint encouragement. A digital vision board is especially helpful for people who travel often or work mostly online.

For a digital board, you can use apps like Canva, Pinterest, or Trello. These platforms allow you to store images, Bible verses, and even videos or songs that inspire you.

Some people choose to use both—a digital board for on-the-go reminders and a physical board for a strong presence at home.

3. Select Meaningful Images and Words

When choosing what to place on your vision board, focus on images, symbols, and words that deeply connect with your faith, values, and life purpose. Do not just look for something that is nice to see. Choose visuals that stir your heart, inspire hope, and remind you of God's promises. Every picture should have meaning and speak to your spirit in a personal way.

For example, if you have a goal related to your faith, you might include a Bible, an image of praying hands, or a picture of a church community worshipping together. For family goals, you could use smiling family portraits, a warm home, or pictures of destinations you hope to visit for family vacations. Ministry goals might include photos of outreach programs, people serving the needy, or missionary trips. If you have personal growth goals, you could add pictures of books, a graduation cap, or images of a healthy lifestyle.

It is also powerful to include Bible verses that encourage and strengthen you. Scriptures like *"For I know the plans I have for you..."* **(Jeremiah 29:11)** or *"The Lord will fight for you; you need only to be still"* **(Exodus 14:14)** can speak directly to your spirit whenever you see them.

The images and words you choose should not only represent what you want to achieve, but also remind you daily that God is with you in the journey toward those dreams.

4. Arrange and Design

Once you have gathered all your images, words, and verses, it is time to arrange them on your vision board in a way that is clear and inspiring. Place your most important goals in the centre of the board so they are the first thing your eyes see. Surround them with the other goals that support and connect to your main vision.

You can create sections for different areas of your life, such as faith, family, career, health, ministry, and personal development. This helps you see balance in your life and reminds you that God cares about every part of it. For example, the faith section could have Bible verses and worship images, while the health section could include healthy food pictures, exercise goals, and reminders to care for your body as God's temple.

Think about the overall design. Use colours, shapes, and arrangements that feel joyful and hopeful to you. You might group similar themes together or use a flow that guides your eyes from one dream to another. Make sure every item reflects your trust in God's promises and serves as a daily reminder that your life is in His hands.

Your vision board should not just be a collection of random pictures—it should be a visual prayer, filled with faith and intention.

5. Be Adaptive

"For we know in part and we prophesy in part. But when that which is perfect has come, then that which is in part will be done away." — ***1 Corinthians 13:9–10***

Life is always changing, and so should your vision board. God often reveals His plan step by step, not all at once. What you see today may only be a part of the bigger picture He is preparing for you. That is why it is important to stay flexible and open to His guidance.

We live in a world where things change rapidly. New technologies, tools, and ideas appear overnight, and sometimes they open unexpected doors for you to achieve your goals in a faster or better way. For example, new AI models, apps, and software can make your work easier and save you time, giving you more space to focus on your calling.

Being adaptive does not mean abandoning your vision; it means being willing to adjust the methods and tools you use to get there. If something becomes outdated or irrelevant, replace it without fear. Keep asking God for wisdom on what to keep, what to remove, and what to add.

Your vision board should grow with you. As you learn more, as God reveals more, and as life changes, update it so it continues to reflect His will for your life. Think of it as a living document of your journey with God—always moving, always growing, always guided by

His hand.

Maintaining Focus Through Daily and Weekly Review

Place your vision board somewhere you will see it often—such as in your bedroom, your workspace, or even as your phone wallpaper if it is digital. The goal is to keep your vision in front of you, so it becomes a constant reminder of what God has placed in your heart.

Set aside a few minutes each day or at least once a week to pause and truly focus on your board. Look at each picture, word, or verse and let it speak to you again. Use this time to pray over your goals, thank God for the progress you have made, and ask Him to renew your faith where it may have weakened.

This regular review keeps your vision alive. It helps you stay committed, especially when life gets busy or when challenges come. It also strengthens your belief that what you see will one day become reality.

Think of your vision board as a spiritual anchor—when distractions or doubts arise, these moments of review pull you back to your purpose and remind you of the promises God has made for your life.

Keeping Your Vision Board God-Centered

When creating a vision board, it is easy to let personal desires take the lead and slowly drift into self-focused wishes. This happens when we focus more on what will make us look good rather than what will glorify God. A God-centered vision board is different—it is rooted in biblical truth and aligned with His will.

Before adding anything to your board, pause and measure it against Scripture. Ask yourself: Does this goal glorify God? Will it bless others? Is it about building His kingdom or just building my comfort? This mindset shifts the focus from self-promotion to God's purpose.

Make sure your board includes spiritual goals alongside material ones. For example, discipleship, deepening your prayer life, serving in your community, giving generously, and sharing the gospel are all God-honouring visions.

When your board is centred on God, it becomes an act of worship rather than wish-making. It reminds you daily that your dreams are not just for your own benefit, but to advance God's plans and bring light to others. This approach not only keeps your heart humble but also invites God's favour over your journey.

Avoiding Discouragement When the Vision Takes Time

A vision board is a tool to keep your focus clear, but it is not a magic solution that makes things happen instantly. God works according to His perfect timing, and sometimes that timing is very different from what we expect. The Bible reminds us,

"For the vision is yet for an appointed time... Though it tarries, wait for it; because it will surely come" ***(Habakkuk 2:3).***

Look at the lives of Abraham and Jacob—they waited many years before God's promises were fulfilled. Their seasons of waiting were not wasted; they were times of growth, trust, and preparation. In the same way, when progress feels slow, shift your heart toward gratitude for what God has already done.

Waiting seasons can be opportunities to deepen your faith, refine your character, and gain wisdom. Instead of giving in to discouragement, use these moments to pray, listen for God's guidance, and remain open to His "different but better" answers.

When we remember that God is always faithful, delays lose their power to make us doubt. His timing is not just perfect—it is purposeful, designed to prepare us for the fullness of the blessing He has planned.

Adding a Progress Tracker to Your Vision

A progress tracker is a simple but powerful way to see how far you have come toward your goals and to know what still lies ahead. By recording each achievement—whether it is a big milestone or a small step—you give yourself a reason to celebrate progress along the way.

This tracker could take many forms: a checklist placed next to your vision board, a journal where you record victories, a calendar marking milestones, or even a digital app that visually shows your growth. Whatever the method, seeing progress with your own eyes can be deeply encouraging.

When growth feels slow, remember that slow growth is still growth. Each step matters. Looking at your tracker during moments of tiredness or doubt can reignite your motivation and remind you that God has been helping you every step of the way.

"Do not despise these small beginnings, for the Lord rejoices to see the work begin" - ***Zechariah 4:10***

Every action you take in faith is a step toward the fulfilment of your vision. Tracking that journey not only builds your confidence, it strengthens your trust in God's faithfulness for the road ahead.

Pairing Your Vision Board with Prayer, Fasting, and Accountability

A vision board becomes far more powerful when it is supported by spiritual disciplines. Prayer keeps your heart aligned with God's will, fasting sharpens your focus and faith, and accountability helps you stay committed even when the journey is long or difficult.

Pray regularly over the dreams and goals displayed on your board. Ask God for wisdom, direction, and the strength to persevere. If you are seeking a breakthrough, deeper clarity, or spiritual renewal, consider setting aside time for fasting. This act of sacrifice can help you draw closer to God and hear His voice more clearly.

Share your vision board with a trusted friend, mentor, or prayer partner. Having someone walk alongside you allows for mutual encouragement, honest feedback, and shared celebration of progress—no matter how small. The Bible reminds us,

"Two are better than one, because they have a good reward for their toil. For if they fall, one will lift up his fellow" - ***Ecclesiastes 4:9–10***

When prayer, fasting, and accountability are paired with your vision board, your goals are no longer just personal ambitions—they become a journey of faith, obedience, and partnership with God.

Chapter 5

To-Do Systems

To achieve our goals, whether they are daily tasks or long-term ambitions, we need an effective to-do system. In this chapter, we will look at practical methods and simple approaches for creating and managing to-do lists that truly help you move forward. From organizing your daily priorities to applying strategies from productivity research, you will learn how to build a system that keeps you focused, motivated, and clear as you work toward both small wins and big life goals.

To-Do Systems: Digital vs Paper

Digital To-Do Systems – Digital to-do lists use apps or software to help you organize and track your tasks. Popular tools include Todoist, Microsoft To Do, Google Keep, and Notion. These systems allow you to add, edit, and manage tasks from your phone, tablet, or computer.

Pros: One of the biggest advantages of digital systems is mobility. You can check your tasks anywhere as long as you have your device with you. Many apps also provide reminders and notifications so you do not forget deadlines or important meetings. Another strength is integration. Digital lists can connect with your calendar, email, and even team collaboration tools, making it easy to manage work and personal life in one place. Digital systems are also highly editable. You can rearrange priorities, create new categories, or mark tasks as completed with just a few taps.

Cons: At the same time, digital systems have their challenges. Using a phone or computer for task management can be distracting because of notifications from social media or other apps. Some apps are packed with too many features, which may lead you to spend more time setting up the system than actually completing tasks. There is also dependence on technology. If your battery dies, the internet is down, or syncing fails, your planning process may be interrupted.

Paper To-Do Systems – Paper-based systems include handwritten lists, planners, diaries, or even sticky notes. Many people prefer this method because of its simplicity and the satisfying feeling of writing things down.

Pros: Writing by hand has cognitive benefits. It activates the brain's reticular activating system (RAS), which helps improve focus, attention, and memory. This means you may retain your tasks better and feel clearer about your priorities. Another benefit is the sense of satisfaction. Crossing off a completed task on paper gives a rewarding feeling that many people find motivating. Paper systems are also simple. You do not need to learn new software or worry about device issues or distractions.

Cons: Paper systems also have limits. They are less portable because you need to carry your notebook or planner with you wherever you go. They do not provide automatic reminders, alarms, or calendar integration, which means you must rely fully on your memory. Editing lists can also be inconvenient, as rearranging or moving tasks often requires rewriting them.

Which Should You Use?

Both systems have their own strengths, and the choice often depends on your lifestyle and work style. Writing with pen and paper can sharpen focus and memory, while digital apps bring convenience and flexibility. The best approach may be to combine the two.

For example, you can capture all your tasks in a digital app like Todoist or Microsoft To Do so you always have access to them. Then, each morning or when you arrive at your workspace, write down your top three to five tasks on a piece of paper or in a notebook. This act of writing focuses your mind on the day's priorities, while the digital system keeps everything organized and backed up. By using both methods together, you get the mental clarity of handwriting and the practical convenience of technology.

PTT – Plan Tomorrow Today

PTT, which stands for Plan Tomorrow Today, is one of the most effective ways to stay productive and focused. The idea is simple: before you go to bed at night, you take a few minutes to outline your tasks and priorities for the next day. By doing this, you free your mornings from decision-making and instead use your highest energy for action.

Your brain is like a powerhouse. When you sleep well, your mental energy is restored to its peak level. The first few hours after waking up are when your mind is the clearest and sharpest. If you spend that fresh energy deciding what to do, you waste the best part of your day on planning instead of doing. By planning your tasks the night before, you wake up ready to act on your list without hesitation.

For example, imagine two people. One wakes up and spends 30 minutes thinking about what to do, shuffling tasks, and checking messages. The other wakes up and immediately starts with the top three tasks they planned the night before. The second person is already ahead while the first is still figuring things out. This is the power of PTT.

Planning before bed does more than just save time. When you write down your tasks for tomorrow, your mind feels lighter and less cluttered. This allows you to sleep more peacefully because you no longer have to keep reminding yourself of what needs to be done.

Another benefit is how your subconscious works during sleep. While your body rests, your mind continues processing ideas in the background. Many people find that solutions, fresh ideas, or clarity about a problem often come in the morning after they have written down their plans the night before.

There is also a spiritual side to this practice. Before sleeping, you can pray over your plans and surrender them to God. The Bible says, "Commit to the Lord whatever you do, and he will establish your plans" (Proverbs 16:3). Isaiah 45:2 adds, "I will go before you and make the crooked places straight." When you plan with prayer, you are not only preparing your mind but also inviting God's guidance for the day ahead. You may not know the challenges or opportunities tomorrow will bring, but by partnering with God in your planning, you can walk with more peace and confidence.

What If You Cannot Plan Everything?

Not every job or lifestyle allows you to know tomorrow's tasks in advance. Some work depends on real-time data, client requests, or information that only comes in the morning. In this case, the PTT method still works. You can plan the tasks that you already know and leave space in your schedule for new priorities.

For example, you can block out time in your calendar as "flexible work" or "to be filled." This way, you start your day with a framework instead of a blank page, and you still have room to adjust as new information arrives. The goal is not to predict everything perfectly but to give yourself a running start.

How to Practice PTT

1. Choose a tool – Decide how you want to capture your tasks. If you like the feeling of writing by hand, you can use a notebook, a daily planner, or even sticky notes.

Handwriting often gives a sense of connection and clarity. If you prefer technology, digital apps like Todoist, Microsoft To Do, Notion, or Google Keep are excellent options. These apps let you set reminders, organize tasks by category, and sync across devices so you can access your plan anywhere. The tool you choose does not matter as much as your consistency in using it.

2. Spend 5 to 10 minutes at night – Before going to bed, set aside a few quiet minutes to plan your next day. This does not need to be complicated. Simply write down the tasks you already know you need to complete tomorrow. Think about your meetings, deadlines, personal commitments, and even small errands. Keeping it simple helps you create a clear picture of your day without overwhelming yourself. This short investment of time can save you from confusion and wasted energy the next morning.

3. Highlight your top 3 tasks – Once you have written your list, pick the three most important tasks for the next day. These should be the tasks that, if completed, will make you feel your day was successful. You can circle them, mark them with a star, or even list them separately at the top of the page. Focusing on three key tasks prevents overwhelm and ensures you spend your best energy on what really matters, instead of getting lost in small or less important activities.

4. Pray or reflect – Take a quiet moment to reflect on your plan. If you are spiritual, you can pray over your list, asking for strength, wisdom, and guidance for the day ahead. The Bible says, "Commit to the Lord whatever you do, and he will establish your plans" (Proverbs 16:3). This step not only calms your mind but also gives you confidence that you are not facing tomorrow alone. Even if you are not spiritual, simply pausing to breathe, visualize your next day, or mentally prepare yourself creates peace and focus before sleep.

5. Review in the morning – When you wake up, do not waste your peak energy on figuring out what needs to be done. Instead, look at your prepared list and begin your day with action. Start with one of your top three tasks and build momentum. This way, you are using your clearest and freshest energy for doing meaningful work rather than for planning.

Planning your day the night before is a small habit with big results. It allows you to use your mornings for high-value work, reduces stress, and creates a sense of clarity. It also gives your mind and spirit a chance to prepare overnight. Even if your schedule is unpredictable, PTT helps you stay proactive and adaptable. Instead of letting the day control you, you begin each morning already in control.

The ABCDE Method

To make progress in life, it is not enough to simply stay busy. Many people fill their days with activity but still feel unfulfilled because they are not focusing on what truly matters. The ABCDE Method is a simple and powerful way to prioritize your daily tasks so that your time and energy are spent wisely. This method helps you separate the important from the unimportant, ensuring that the hours God gives you each day are used to make the greatest impact.

How the ABCDE Method Works

The ABCDE Method begins with writing down your daily tasks. Once you have your list, assign each task a letter from A, B, C, D, or E, based on its level of importance and the consequences of completing or not completing it.

- **A Tasks:** These are the tasks you must do. They carry serious consequences if left undone and are often the most important things in your day. Completing them brings great progress, while neglecting them can bring serious setbacks.
- **B Tasks:** These are things you should do. They matter, but the consequences of delay or neglect are mild compared to A tasks. These should never come before your A tasks.
- **C Tasks:** These are things that are nice to do, but there are no real consequences if you do them or not. They can wait.
- **D Tasks:** These are tasks you can delegate to someone else. If another person can handle them, especially if it frees up your time for higher priorities, let them take care of it.
- **E Tasks:** These are tasks you can eliminate. They bring no value, and keeping them on your list only clutters your mind.

Once you assign the letters, you then number them in order of priority: A-1, A-2, A-3, and so on. The key is to begin with your **A-1 task** and focus on it until it is complete. As Scripture reminds us, *"Let all things be done decently and in order"* **(1 Corinthians 14:40)**. Order brings clarity, and clarity leads to fruitful results.

Example Scenarios Using the ABCDE Method

Work Example – John the Manager John, a team manager, makes his list of tasks. Preparing a client presentation is marked as an **A task** because if it is late, the client may lose trust. Approving leave requests becomes a **B task**, as it is important but not critical. Replying to social emails is a **C task**, since it has no real consequences. Arranging a team lunch is a **D task** that can be delegated to his assistant. Finally, reviewing old project files is an **E task**, which he can eliminate. John begins his day with the client presentation, his **A-1 task**, ensuring his most important responsibility is handled first.

Personal Example – Grace the Writer Grace, who is writing her novel, organizes her day using the method. Writing 1,000 new words is her **A task**, since it directly advances her manuscript. Research for future chapters becomes a **B task**, as it is helpful but not urgent today. Organizing digital notes is marked as a **C task**, and asking a friend for feedback is a **D task** she can delegate. Reviewing old story ideas is an **E task** she decides to eliminate. Grace focuses on her A task first, knowing that consistent progress on her writing is what truly matters.

Study Example – Alex the Student Alex, a student preparing for exams, plans his study session. Reviewing the toughest chapter for tomorrow's test is his **A task** because it directly impacts his performance. Updating class notes is a **B task**, and chatting with friends about the test is a **C task**. Photocopying study material is a **D task** that he can ask a classmate to help with. Checking last year's attendance sheet is an **E task** with no value. Alex devotes his best energy to reviewing the tough chapter first, giving him confidence for his exam.

Common Mistakes to Avoid When Prioritizing

When people fail with prioritization, it is often because they fall into certain traps. One mistake is **confusing activity with productivity**. Being busy with B and C tasks may feel satisfying, but it does not create meaningful results. Another mistake is **neglecting delegation**. Trying to do everything alone wastes time that could be spent on higher-value work. Some also fail to **eliminate unneeded tasks**, carrying around responsibilities that no longer matter. Others attempt to **multitask on A items**, splitting their attention and slowing progress. Another trap is **improper grouping**, treating C tasks as if they are A tasks. Finally, some fail to **re-prioritize**. Life changes daily, and what mattered yesterday may not matter today. Without regular review, your system quickly becomes outdated.

The ABCDE Method teaches us that not all tasks are equal. As Jesus Himself reminded Martha, "*You are worried and upset about many things, but few things are needed—or indeed only one*" **(Luke 10:41-42).**

True productivity comes from knowing what matters most and giving it our full attention.

When you apply this method with discipline, you stop wasting time on things that bring little value and start investing in what brings lasting results. Over time, this habit can double or even triple your effectiveness. More importantly, it allows you to honor God with your time, focusing on the tasks that align with your purpose.

By practicing the ABCDE Method, you will not only get more done but also find greater peace and fulfillment, knowing that your daily work is meaningful and guided by order, clarity, and God's wisdom.

The Law of Three

The Law of Three is a powerful principle of productivity. It teaches that out of all the tasks you could possibly do in a day, only three truly matter. These three tasks produce most of the value in your work—sometimes as much as 90 percent. No matter how long your to-do list may be, your real impact comes from just a few essential activities. When you learn to focus on these, you step into greater clarity, success, and fulfillment.

Understanding the Law of Three

If we look at our long list of 30, 40, or even 50 tasks in a week, we will soon realize something surprising. Out of all those activities, only three per day activities truly create the greatest value for our work, our organization, and even our personal growth. The rest, though they may feel urgent or necessary, contribute only a small portion of real impact. The secret to true productivity is learning to recognize these three most important tasks and focusing our best energy on them.

How to Find Your Top Three

Start by writing down every task you do in your role, whether it is for a day, a week, or a month. Once you have your list, ask yourself three questions:

1. If I could only do one thing on this list all day, which activity would bring the greatest value to my work and my company?
2. If I could do a second thing, which task would add the next highest value?
3. If I could only do one more task, which third activity would still make the biggest difference?

Circle or highlight your answers. These are your "big three." Everything else still has importance, but not the same weight. If you focus on completing these three each day, your effectiveness will grow faster than you imagine.

Four Lessons from the Law of Three

The Law of Three comes with four powerful lessons:

1. **Do fewer things.** You will never finish everything on your list. Learn to stop giving energy to the countless small and less important tasks.
2. **Do more important things.** Focus on the top three and complete them first. This alone will transform your productivity.

3. **Do them most of the time.** The more hours you invest in your top tasks, the more results you will see and the more peace you will feel inside.
4. **Get better at them.** Commit to growing in the skills that matter most. When you improve at your top three, your value multiplies, and so does your confidence.

Staying Focused on Your Priorities

Once you identify your three, you need strategies to keep them in focus:

- **Schedule deep work times.** Give yourself blocks of uninterrupted time where you work only on your top tasks. Put away distractions.
- **Batch or cut small tasks.** Group minor chores together and handle them quickly, or delegate and eliminate them where possible.
- **Review daily.** Each morning, check your list of three before you start. If new tasks come in, weigh them carefully before shifting priorities.
- **Keep reminders visible.** Write your three on sticky notes, make them your phone wallpaper, or highlight them in your planner.
- **Set boundaries.** Tell others when you need focused time, so they respect your space.
- **Celebrate completion.** When you finish a major task, thank God, rejoice, and let it motivate you to keep going.

The Long-Term Power of the Law of Three

When you practice the Law of Three every day, progress toward your biggest goals becomes certain. Instead of scattering your time and attention on too many things, you begin to invest your energy where it matters most. Over time, this simple daily habit creates a compounding effect. Little by little, the consistent focus adds up. You start noticing greater results in your career, deeper satisfaction in your work, and a stronger sense of peace in your personal life.

By focusing on your top three, you achieve three powerful benefits. First, you move the needle on your most important projects. Second, you build expertise and mastery that set you apart from others. And third, you reduce stress, because you learn to let go of the unimportant tasks that do not add real value.

Make a decision today: decide that you will become the hardest working and most productive person in your organization. Do not announce it to others. Do not boast about it. Imagine there is a silent contest for productivity, and only you know about it. Let your actions speak. Let your results be the proof. As Scripture says, "*Whatever you do, work at it with all your heart, as working for the Lord, not for men.*"?

When you work this way, with focus, excellence, and faithfulness, people will notice. But more importantly, you will know that you have offered your very best to God and to the calling He has placed on your life.

Time Blocking and Scheduling

"See then that you walk circumspectly, not as fools but as wise, redeeming the time, because the days are evil."

— Ephesians 5:15–16

In this verse, Paul reminds us to redeem the time and to use it wisely. When I was praying and thinking about time before writing this topic, the Holy Spirit gave me a clear perspective. For the world, time management is simply about being efficient or getting more things done. But for us as believers, it carries a deeper responsibility.

We are called to study the Word of God, spend time in prayer, attend church services, and join fasting and prayer meetings, all while still fulfilling our work and family responsibilities. For many people in the world, endlessly scrolling on social media or binge-watching shows may seem normal. But for us, as children of God, our priority is different. Jesus taught us to seek first the Kingdom of God. Our time should be invested in building a strong relationship with Him and living out the purpose He has called us to.

Paul again said in ***Colossians 4:5*** *"Walk in wisdom toward those who are outside, redeeming the time."* This shows us that time is a gift from God, and it must be used with wisdom. Time blocking and scheduling are powerful tools that can help us use the 24 hours God gives each day in a way that honours Him and strengthens both our spiritual and daily life.

Integrating To-Dos into Time Blocks – Time blocking means dividing your day into clear segments of time, each dedicated to a specific task or type of work. Instead of only writing a list of what needs to be done, you decide when you will do it. For example, you might block one hour in the morning for prayer and reflection, two hours for focused work, and thirty minutes for family calls. This approach removes the stress of constant decision-making during the day. When the time comes, you already know what to do, and you can give your full attention without distraction.

Using Calendars with To-Do Lists – To make time blocking more effective, combine your to-do list with a calendar. Begin by identifying your most important tasks for the day. Then, assign specific time slots for them on your calendar. Digital tools like Google Calendar, Microsoft Outlook, or Apple Calendar are very useful for this. You can also use paper planners if you prefer writing things down. When you see your tasks laid out on a calendar, you gain a clear picture of your commitments. It prevents you from overloading your schedule and helps you avoid multitasking, which often leads to stress and poor results.

Adapting Time Blocks for Unexpected Changes – Life is full of surprises, and interruptions often come when we least expect them. To stay productive, create buffer times between your major tasks. These small gaps allow space for urgent needs, short breaks, or catching up on something you could not finish earlier. If something truly urgent comes up, do not panic. Simply move the task you missed to another block of time. Flexibility is essential. At the end of the day, review your calendar and shift any unfinished tasks to tomorrow. This keeps you steady and helps you trust that you are still moving forward, even when plans change.

Chunking Tasks by Project, Context, or Time Needed – Another way to use time blocking wisely is to group similar tasks together. This helps you stay focused and avoid wasting energy on switching between different types of work. You can group tasks by project, such as setting aside two hours to work only on a major report. You can also group by context, such as making all your phone calls in one block of time. Finally, you can group by the time required. Use short blocks, sometimes called "power hours," for quick tasks, and set aside longer blocks for deep, focused work like writing, planning, or study.

Using Colour Coding and Tags – Visual clarity makes time blocking easier to follow. You can assign colours to your calendar blocks to see priorities at a glance. For example, you might use red for urgent tasks, blue for meetings, green for personal or spiritual growth, and yellow for family time. Many apps like Google Calendar or Notion allow this feature. You can also use tags or categories in to-do list apps, labelling tasks like “emails,” “errands,” or “study.” This way, your mind quickly understands what each block represents without extra effort.

When you practice time blocking with discipline and prayer, you begin to live with more clarity, peace, and purpose. You no longer just hope to fit in what matters—you intentionally make room for it. In this way, your days are ordered, your energy is protected, and your focus remains on the tasks that truly honour God and bless your life.

Buffer Time

Buffer time means leaving open spaces in your schedule to handle unexpected delays, interruptions, or changes. In today's world, distractions come from every direction—notifications, surprise visitors, urgent phone calls, or even shifts in our own mood and energy. Because of this, rigid schedules often collapse when real life shows up. Buffer time acts like a safety net. It helps you stay on track without losing peace, even when things do not go exactly as planned.

As believers, we sometimes face unexpected spiritual needs as well. There may be days when the Spirit leads us to spend more time in prayer or in the Word. These are precious moments, but they may not fit neatly into our fixed schedule. Without buffer time, such events can push important tasks into tomorrow and create unnecessary stress. But when we include a buffer, we allow space for God's leading and for the unexpected demands of life.

For example, imagine you set a goal to finish reading a book in one month. If you plan for all 30 days, then missing even a few days may cause you to fall behind. Instead, if you plan to finish in 25 days and leave a 5-day buffer, you have built-in grace. Those extra days absorb interruptions—whether missed reading sessions, sudden commitments, or days when you feel led to focus more on prayer—without ruining your progress.

Buffer time can be applied in different ways. In your day-to-day plan, leave small gaps between tasks or allow open space after focused work. This gives you room to recover if something takes longer than expected. Avoid packing your week too tightly. Keep an evening or even a full day unscheduled for catching up, emergencies, or rest. For long-term goals, include buffer days in your timeline. These "grace periods" make your plan flexible and forgiving when life interrupts.

The benefits of buffer time are powerful. It reduces stress and pressure when things do not go as planned. It helps you recover from distractions without losing momentum. It makes your goals more realistic and easier to achieve. It also gives space for rest, meaningful moments, and even spiritual focus when God calls you to pause.

By practising buffer time, you design your schedule in a way that allows success even when life happens. You no longer live under the burden of perfection but with the wisdom of preparation.

The Pomodoro Technique

The Pomodoro Technique is a simple yet powerful way to manage your time. It was developed by Francesco Cirillo in the late 1980s, and today it is used by people all over the world. The main idea is to divide your work into short, focused intervals of effort, followed by short breaks. These intervals are called ***"pomodoros."***

Traditionally, each pomodoro lasts for 25 minutes. You work with full focus during this time, giving your complete attention to one task. When the 25 minutes are over, you take a 5-minute break to rest your mind and body. After completing four pomodoros, you take a longer break of about 15 to 30 minutes to recharge before starting again. This creates a rhythm of work and rest that keeps you fresh and productive.

You can adjust the length of the intervals to match your stamina. Some people prefer 25 minutes, while others find 40 minutes works better for them. The key is to stay consistent: work with full focus during the set time, then step away for a break before starting again.

This method offers many benefits. It improves focus by training your mind to give undivided attention to the present moment. It prevents burnout by making sure you rest before exhaustion sets in. It makes big tasks feel less overwhelming by breaking them into smaller steps. It also builds motivation because you can see how much progress you make, pomodoro by pomodoro.

To get started, you do not need anything complicated. A simple timer on your phone or even a kitchen timer will work. Today, there are also many apps that give you flexibility and send a notification when a pomodoro ends. During each work session, remove distractions. Do not check emails, scroll through social media, or multitask. Let that time belong fully to the task before you. Use your short breaks for something refreshing, like stretching, walking, or deep breathing.

The Pomodoro Technique is especially useful for those who struggle with procrastination, feel overwhelmed by large projects, or desire a steady rhythm to their day. It creates balance, where work and rest go hand in hand. This balance reminds us of the wisdom of God, who designed us to need both focus and renewal. Even in creation, He set apart the Sabbath as a rhythm of rest after work.

When you embrace this technique, you are not just learning to manage time better—you are practicing a lifestyle of focus, discipline, and healthy rest.

Reviewing and Reflecting System

One of the most powerful habits you can build for lasting productivity is reviewing and reflecting at the end of each day. This practice takes only five to ten minutes, but the impact is life-changing.

Begin by looking at your to-do list. Mark the tasks you have completed, carry forward the ones that are unfinished, and prayerfully readjust your priorities for tomorrow. This keeps your planning system flexible and alive, rather than rigid and lifeless.

As you reflect, ask yourself: *What worked well today? Where was I interrupted? What can I do better tomorrow?* Then make small adjustments in your schedule and priorities for the next day. This simple review helps you quickly identify distractions, see what slows you down, and make necessary changes before the same problems repeat.

It is also important to feed your progress into a journal, a tracker sheet, or a productivity app. Document major events, setbacks, and achievements. Mistakes will teach you valuable lessons for the future, while recording achievements will give you motivation when you face challenges again.

Think of David before he fought Goliath. He reminded himself of how God had delivered him from the lion and the bear, He said to King Saul "*The Lord who delivered me from the paw of the lion and from the paw of the bear, He will deliver me from the hand of this Philistine*" ***(1 Samuel 17:37).*** David had no notebook or app to record his victories, but he carried them in his heart. Today, God has given us the tools to record these things in writing. By keeping a record of your daily progress, struggles, and wins, you will have something to return to for encouragement and growth.

Finally, end each day with this question: "*If I were given this same day again, what would I do differently?*" This single question will make you more aware of small mistakes you might have ignored, and it will push you toward continual improvement. Over time, this habit will grow your self-awareness, sharpen your decisions, and help you use your time more effectively for God's glory.

My To-Do List Organization

After several years of trial and improvement, I created a booklet system that helps me stay consistent and focused. The booklet is divided into four quarters, each covering three months.

Every month begins with a **Monthly Goal Setting** page, where I write down my key focus areas and priorities for the month. After that, the booklet moves into the **daily to-do pages**.

On each daily page, I have six fixed tasks that I repeat every day. Instead of writing them again and again, I use printed icons to represent them. Below that, there are seven blank lines for additional to-do items, each with a checkbox to mark completion.

At the bottom of the page, I have included a short reflecting question. This small habit keeps me aware of how I am spending my time and helps me grow a little each day.

At the end of every month, I have a **Monthly Review** page. This is where I slow down and look back on the month that has passed. On this page, I write down my **accounting**, the important **events** that happened, and the **memories** I want to keep. I also note the **best thought** or idea I came across during the month, along with any **major decisions** I made.

Finally, I include a section called **Photo of the Month**, where I place one picture that captures the heart of that month. This makes the review not just practical, but also personal and meaningful.

Chapter 6

Declarations: Speaking Life

Three Dimensions of Laws

There are different levels of laws that govern the universe. Our spiritual father, **Apostle Dr. Alph Lukau** once taught us, *"The Kingdom of God operates in two aspects: Dimensions and Seasons."* This truth opened my eyes to understand why in today's world we constantly hear about affirmations, manifestations, and what people call the "law of attraction." Social media, self-help books, coaching videos, and motivational reels are filled with these teachings. Thousands of people testify that they manifested what they wanted simply by affirming and speaking it.

As a born-again child of God, I was honestly curious and at times even envious. I wondered what really makes us different from non-believers if they too receive results by following these principles. Was eternal life the only difference, or was there something deeper, especially about the power of speaking that belonged only to God's children?

In that moment of questioning, the Holy Spirit reminded me of the words of Scripture: *"Do not fret because of evildoers, nor be envious of the wicked"* - ***Proverbs 24:19*** and ***Psalm 37:1–3***

Still, I wanted to understand what **'the exclusivity of the children of God'** really was in this area of speaking. Then the Lord gave me a revelation of three dimensions of laws.

1. Natural Laws

The first dimension is natural laws. These are the basic principles that govern the physical universe. They operate without partiality and apply to everyone and everything—human beings, animals, or even objects—regardless of faith or belief. Gravity is one such law. Whether a believer or non-believer jumps from a building, the law of gravity will pull both down. The rotation of the earth producing day and night is another. These laws keep order in creation and ensure that life functions consistently.

The Bible also affirms the existence of these fixed patterns. In ***Jeremiah 33:25***, the Lord says, *"If My covenant is not with day and night, and if I have not appointed the ordinances of heaven and earth..."* These natural ordinances are the lowest level of laws, yet they provide a stable foundation for life on earth.

2. Spiritual Laws

The second dimension is spiritual laws. The world often calls them ***"universal laws."*** They include principles like sowing and reaping, the power of words, and even generosity. These laws are not confined to believers alone. They work for anyone who applies them, regardless of religion or background.

The book of Proverbs is filled with spiritual laws, and much of modern positivity culture has sprung from these very principles. For example, *"For as he thinks in his heart, so is he"* - ***Proverbs 23:7*** is the foundation of what is now called **"positive thinking."** Many well-known classic self-help books, such as **Think and Grow Rich** and **The Power of Your Subconscious Mind**, are built upon these laws. When someone consistently speaks positive words *(They call it affirmations)*, whether they are a believer or not, they usually see positive outcomes. Even the ***tithing*** falls under spiritual laws, which is why many religions observe it nowadays and experience blessings through it. Fasting, building altars, and similar practices also operate under spiritual laws.

This is why people who practice affirmations, visualization, or generosity often experience results. They are unknowingly applying spiritual laws that God Himself established. The laws are built into the fabric of creation and respond to faith, words, and actions—even if the person does not acknowledge the Lord.

3. God's Laws (Covenant Laws)

The highest dimension is God's Laws, also called ***covenant laws***. These are reserved exclusively for the children of God—those who have confessed Jesus Christ as Lord and are redeemed by His blood. This level is not simply about principles but about covenant relationship.

The Bible says in ***Romans 10:9***, *"If you confess with your mouth the Lord Jesus and believe in your heart that God has raised Him from the dead, you will be saved."* Once redeemed, the believer's name is written in the Lamb's Book of Life as ***Revelation 21:27*** says: *"But there shall by no means enter it anything that defiles, or causes an abomination or a lie, but only those who are written in the Lamb's Book of Life."*

Along with salvation, God's children are given authority. *The Word says, "And these signs will follow those who believe: In My name they will cast out demons; they will speak with new tongues; they will take up serpents; and if they drink anything deadly, it will by no means hurt them; they will lay hands on the sick, and they will recover"* - ***Mark 16:17–18***. *In addition, Jesus declared, "Behold, I give you the authority to trample on serpents and scorpions, and over all the power of the enemy, and nothing shall by any means hurt you"* - ***Luke 10:19***. These promises reveal the true exclusivity of the children of God.

This is a realm where declarations are no longer just affirmations or universal principles but divine decrees backed by the authority of heaven. ***Job 22:28*** promises, *"You will also declare a thing, and it will be established for you..."* When non-believers speak positively, their words may operate under spiritual laws, and they may see certain results. But when a believer speaks in alignment with God's Word in the name of Jesus, it is no longer just a principle—it becomes a decree. Heaven itself backs the words, and the outcome carries eternal authority. We are not limited to natural or spiritual laws alone. By covenant, we have access to God's highest laws, which turn our words into decrees that shape reality with divine power.

The Distinction

As we have already discussed, God's laws are exclusive to His children who are born again through Christ. With these laws comes a promise of distinction—a clear separation between those who belong to God and those who do not. It is impossible for a child of God to be left behind or for a non-believer to surpass a believer in the things that truly matter in God's Kingdom.

God's laws secure believers with a unique identity, status, and privilege. This distinction sets apart the children of God from the rest of the world. By covenant, His people have the promise of divine preference, protection, and spiritual authority. This is especially evident when it comes to the power and effect of their words.

In ***Exodus 8:23***, God said to Pharaoh, "*I will make a difference between My people and your people.*" In this statement, God called the Hebrews His people and separated them from the Egyptians. This shows us that from the beginning, God has made a line of difference between His children and those who do not belong to Him.

In the New Covenant, this truth is reinforced with even greater clarity. ***1 Peter 2:9*** says, "*But you are a chosen generation, a royal priesthood, a holy nation, His own special people, that you may proclaim the praises of Him who called you out of darkness into His marvellous light.*" Believers are given a royal identity and are called special people belonging to God Himself. This is not a position we earn, but a privilege that is freely given through faith in Jesus Christ. This unique position gives the believer an edge that the world cannot copy.

The prophet Malachi also spoke about this divine separation. ***Malachi 3:18*** says, "*Then you shall again discern between the righteous and the wicked, between one who serves God and one who does not serve Him.*" God promises that there will always be a visible and spiritual difference that sets apart those who serve Him from those who do not.

This distinction is especially important when it comes to speaking. It is not the same thing when a believer speaks and when a non-believer speaks. Gentiles may use affirmations or principles and sometimes see results because of spiritual laws at work. But the words of a believer, spoken in faith and in the name of Jesus, carry the authority of heaven itself. Decrees, declarations, and prophetic utterances made by God's people are backed by the power of the Holy Spirit.

The distinction between God's people and others is both practical and eternal. It is practical in that God deals with, blesses, and intervenes in the lives of His children in unique ways. It is eternal because His people have a destiny, promises, and an inheritance that no outsider can claim. Children of God cannot be left behind or outgrown by those outside the Kingdom. Their advantage is rooted in Christ and guaranteed by God's eternal promise.

This distinction is not a matter of pride but of privilege. It is given for the purpose of service, for being a witness to the world, and for displaying the glory of God. The separation between the believer and the non-believer is a testimony of God's faithfulness and a reminder that His people are called to live in a higher dimension, carrying His authority and His promises wherever they go.

Affirmations vs Declarations

In continuation of the last topic, it is important to understand the difference between affirmations and declarations. At first, they may look similar because both involve speaking words aloud. But in essence, in source, and in spiritual impact, they are very different.

Affirmations are positive statements that people use to overcome negative thoughts and feelings. They are often practiced in the self-help world as a way to build confidence, reduce fear, or motivate action. Examples include saying, "I am confident," or "I will be successful." The power of affirmations comes mainly through repetition. By speaking them again and again, people try to reshape their beliefs and attitudes through their own willpower and expectation. While affirmations can help with emotional or psychological well-being, they remain limited to human strength.

Declarations are very different. Declarations are not rooted in human effort or self-will but in the Word of God. When a believer declares what God has spoken, those words carry the authority of heaven. For example, saying "I am loved by God" or "God is my strength" is not based on a self-made idea but on God's promises in Scripture. A declaration aligns with God's truth, and when spoken in faith, it becomes more than a statement. It becomes **a prophetic act** that releases spiritual reality.

The Word of God comes to us in two forms. First, it is logos, the written word of God, available to all who read it. But when that written promise becomes personal through faith and revelation, it turns into rhema, the spoken word of God for a specific situation. Logos is the general truth of God's promises, while rhema is God's personal word that brings life and power to an individual circumstance. Jesus said, *"It is the Spirit who gives life; the flesh profits nothing. The words that I speak to you are spirit, and they are life"* - ***John 6:63.*** This shows us that God's Word, when received and spoken in faith, creates life and changes reality.

Declaring in faith is what it means to be prophetic. It is speaking God's promises into your situation with the confidence that His Word is true. For example, when we declare, **"I am rich,"** we are not speaking wishful thinking. We are standing on the truth of ***2 Corinthians 8:9*** which says, *"For you know the grace of our Lord Jesus Christ, that though He was rich, yet* *for your sakes He became poor, that you through His poverty might become rich."* In the same way, when we say, **"I lack no good thing,"** we are not just encouraging ourselves—we are declaring ***Psalm 23:1,*** *"The Lord is my shepherd; I shall not want."* By declaring the Word, we allow God's promises to replace lack with provision, sickness with healing, and fear with peace.

These blessings and privileges are already available in the spiritual realm, but our words bring them into reality. Once **Dad Alph** taught us about **'The Law of Permission'**. Speaking in faith gives permission that allows heaven's truth to manifest in our lives.

However, declarations do not always produce immediate visible results. Sometimes there is waiting, and sometimes God seems silent. In those moments, Scripture encourages us to remain steadfast. ***Hebrews 10:23*** says, *"Let us hold fast the confession of our hope without wavering, for He who promised is faithful."* ***Galatians 6:9*** reminds us, *"And let us not grow weary while doing good, for in due season we shall reap if we do not lose heart."*

The Kingdom of God operates in both dimensions and seasons. ***Ecclesiastes 3:1-4*** tells us, *"To everything there is a season, a time for every purpose under heaven: ... A time to weep, and a time to laugh; a time to mourn, and a time to dance."* Sometimes declarations are spoken out of season, and their manifestation may be delayed. But even during the waiting, God is working behind the scenes. Faith keeps us declaring until the season comes for the promise to appear.

In conclusion, affirmations are human attempts to influence thought and outcomes through repetition, but declarations are Spirit-empowered words that align with God's promises. Affirmations may strengthen the mind, but declarations release heaven's authority. As children of God, we are called to move beyond affirmations into declarations, because our words, spoken in faith, create realities according to the will of God.

Power of Words

The power of words is not only a spiritual truth but also a reality confirmed by science and human experience. Words have the ability to shape mindsets, influence health, build or break relationships, and even affect the physical world around us. Both faith and secular studies point to the fact that what we say can deeply influence the outcomes of our lives.

One well-known example comes from Japanese researcher Dr. Masaru Emoto. He carried out experiments with water by exposing it to different words, emotions, and intentions before freezing it. When positive and encouraging words such as "thank you" or "love" were spoken over the water, the frozen crystals formed beautiful and symmetrical patterns. When negative words such as "hate" or "fool" were used, the crystals became distorted and broken. The simple message is easy to understand: our words carry energy, and that energy produces visible results. Other small studies also suggested that water exposed to positive intentions looked better and more harmonious than untreated water.

Modern science, especially neuroscience, also supports the impact of words. The brain is shaped by repeated speech and thought. Positive words strengthen neural pathways linked with confidence, motivation, and problem-solving. On the other hand, negative words trigger the brain's stress responses, lowering energy, focus, and creativity. This shows in daily life: people who use uplifting and encouraging words are more resilient, more productive, and better at building meaningful relationships.

The self-help world has embraced this truth as well. It teaches that affirmations such as "I am confident," "I attract abundance," or "I am worthy of love" can transform the way people think and live. Many testify that speaking such words daily gives them hope, courage, and a sense of purpose. But the Bible shows us something even greater: declarations that are rooted in the Word of God are not just self-talk. They carry divine authority.

Scripture is full of wisdom about the power of words. ***Proverbs 16:24*** says, "*Pleasant words are like a honeycomb, Sweetness to the soul and health to the bones.*" Kind and uplifting words bring inner healing and hope. ***Proverbs 12:18*** teaches, "*But the tongue of the wise promotes health.*" Wise and loving words can strengthen someone's spirit and even bring physical healing. Above all, ***Proverbs 18:21*** declares, "*Death and life are in the power of the tongue, And those who love it will eat its fruit.*" This means that our words create outcomes—whether good or bad. Words can heal or wound, build or destroy, bless or curse.

Psychological research agrees that words shape motivation and performance. Positive words release hope and clarity, while negative words spread fear and discouragement. Leaders who speak life into others can inspire teams and create vision. Parents who speak blessing over children plant seeds of confidence. Believers who declare God's promises over their lives open the door for God's power to manifest.

The difference between affirmations and biblical declarations is important. Affirmations rely on human strength and belief. Declarations align with the authority of God's Word and Spirit. When a believer declares God's promises—such as *"The Lord is my shepherd; I shall not want"* ***(Psalm 23:1)*** *or "By His stripes we are healed"* ***(Isaiah 53:5)***—they are not just speaking positive thoughts but activating eternal truths. Declarations remind the believer of God's covenant, shift their mindset toward faith, and release spiritual power that shapes reality.

In daily life, this means choosing words carefully. Speaking encouragement over yourself and others builds perseverance and faith. Declaring God's Word brings clarity of vision, strength in trials, and victory over doubt. Words are not empty—they carry the weight of life and death. As children of God, we are called to use our tongues to speak life, truth, and blessing, so that our lives reflect the glory and power of God.

The Creative Partnership with God

The Bible says in **Titus 1:2** that God *"cannot lie."* **Hebrews 6:18** also affirms that *"it is impossible for God to lie."* Why is this so? Because God is the Creator. Everything that exists was created through His Word. Imagine a situation where there is a yellow ball and God intentionally said it red. What will happen ? the ball would instantly become red. Because His words create reality. Creation itself responds to His voice. This is why lying is impossible for Him. Whatever He declares comes into existence. His very nature is truth, and His Word is final.

As children of God, we share in this creative nature. Genesis teaches that we are made in the image and likeness of God. Part of that likeness includes the ability to speak words that shape outcomes. ***Proverbs 18:21*** says, *"Death and life are in the power of the tongue..."* Our words carry power to build or to destroy, to bless or to curse. This inheritance means that what we say has real effects on our lives, our relationships, and even our environments.

When we speak in alignment with the Word of God, we enter into creative partnership with Him. We are not just repeating human desires or empty affirmations. We are declaring divine promises. This agreement between God's Word and our confession invites His power to work in our lives. Our declarations then become instruments that connect heaven's intent with earthly reality.

Our words can invite God's power into situations. **John 6:63** records Jesus saying, *"The words that I speak to* *you are spirit, and they are life."* Words are not just sounds; they carry spirit and life when they are rooted in God's truth.

As discussed erlier about "**The Law of Permission.**" Our spiritual father explained that God, though all-powerful, chooses not to interfere without our invitation. Speaking His Word gives Him permission to move in our situations. When believers declare Scripture with faith, they open the door for supernatural intervention. This allows God to bring blessing, protection, healing, and breakthrough into their circumstances. On the other hand, the devil, the manipulator, does not respect any law unless it is enforced. The Bible says, "*Resist the devil and he will flee from you.*" He forcefully enters where he is not supposed to be and never leaves without resistance. But how does one resist? By declaring and speaking the Word of God, telling him what is written concerning the situation.

To live as God's children is to recognize this divine partnership. By speaking words of faith in line with Scripture, we honour God, release His creative power, and shape our lives according to His perfect will.

Dangers of Negative Speech

Negative speech is a powerful force. It can shape destinies, destroy relationships, and even hinder the fulfilment of God's promises. The Bible consistently warns about the lasting consequences of words spoken without care or faith. ***Proverbs 13:3*** says, "*He who guards his mouth preserves his life, but he who opens* *wide his lips shall have destruction."* Words are not just fleeting sounds—they carry energy and spiritual influence. They linger over lives and situations, like a cloud affecting outcomes. This is why it is so important to carefully consider what we speak.

In moments of anger, discouragement, or defeat, the temptation to speak negative words is strong. The Israelites provide a clear example. Because they murmured and spoke against God and Moses, they were condemned to wander in the wilderness for forty years, and that generation died without entering the Promised Land **(Numbers 14:26–29)**. Job's wife also reflected the danger of despair when she said to Job, "*Curse God and die!*" ***(Job 2:9).*** Job rebuked her, showing how destructive words of hopelessness can be. The ten spies who gave a fearful report about the Promised Land discouraged Israel, and because of their unbelief, they died by a plague **(Numbers 13:31–33; 14:36–37).** These examples illustrate that negative speech carries real consequences.

Even David, a man after God's own heart, experienced negative speech within himself. In **Psalm 73:2–3,** he admits, "*But as for me, my feet had almost stumbled; My steps had nearly slipped. For I was envious of the boastful, when I saw the prosperity of the wicked."* Yet he corrected his words and focused on God: "*Whom have I in heaven but You? And there is none upon earth that I desire besides You. My flesh and my heart fail; But God is the strength of my heart and my portion forever"* **(Psalm 73:25–26).** Similarly, in **Psalm 55:4–5**, David confesses, "*My heart is severely pained within me, and the terrors of death have fallen upon me;*

Fearfulness and trembling have come upon me, and horror has overwhelmed me." He concludes with faith, saying, *"As for me, I will call upon God, and the Lord shall save me"* **(Psalm 55:16).** This shows believers the importance of acknowledging struggles but finishing with words of faith aligned with God's promises.

The New Testament provides clear instructions about speaking wisely. Paul says, *"Let no corrupt word proceed out of your mouth, but what is good for necessary edification, that it may impart grace to the hearers"* **(Ephesians 4:29).** He also teaches, *"Let your speech always be with grace, seasoned with salt, that you may know how you ought to answer each one"* **(Colossians 4:6).** Our words should not only avoid harm but actively build, encourage, and bless others.

Jesus explained the root of our words in **Matthew 12:34,** *"For out of the abundance of the heart the mouth speaks."* Our speech reflects the condition of our hearts. A heart filled with faith, love, and truth produces life-giving words. A heart filled with bitterness, fear, or doubt produces destructive words. Wise believers monitor both what they speak and what they allow into their hearts, replacing negativity with God's truth and promises.

Being aware of negative speech is essential. Every word carries influence, either inviting blessing or harm. By controlling our tongues, speaking God's truth, and encouraging ourselves and others, we align with God's will and participate in His life-giving work.

Biblical Examples of Speaking Life

The Bible gives many examples of the power of words and how they bring life, blessings, and results. In Genesis, Isaac intended to give Esau the greatest blessing. However, Rebecca, remembering the prophetic word spoken before their birth that "the older shall serve the younger" **(Genesis 25:23)**, prepared food for Jacob and helped him receive the blessing in Esau's place. When Esau returned and sought his father's blessing, Isaac said, "*I have blessed him, and indeed he shall be blessed*" **(Genesis 27:33)**. In those days, blessings were not recorded on paper or in documents; they were spoken words. Once spoken, they could not be undone. The outcomes in the lives of Esau and Jacob later confirmed the power and permanence of those words.

A similar example is seen when Jacob blessed Joseph's sons, Manasseh and Ephraim. Joseph positioned Manasseh, the firstborn, at Jacob's right hand, but Jacob intentionally crossed his hands to place his right hand on Ephraim, the younger, and blessed them **(Genesis 48:13–20)**. This act shows that words spoken in faith and authority carry significance and can alter destiny. Every word has weight and eternal consequence.

David, a man after God's own heart, also demonstrated the power of words. When he confronted Goliath, it was not only his courage but also his declaration in faith that released God's power. David said, "*You come to me with a sword, with a spear, and with a javelin. But I come to you in the name of the Lord of hosts, the God of the armies of Israel, whom you have defied*" **(1 Samuel**

17:45). His words aligned with God's authority and brought victory.

In the ministry of Jesus Christ, the power of words is evident everywhere. People were healed simply by hearing Him speak. Jesus said, *"It is written, 'Man shall not live by bread alone, but by every word of God'"* **(Luke 4:4)**. He often spoke, and healing, deliverance, and miracles followed. **Kenneth E. Hagin** emphasizes this principle in his book ***Hear and Be Healed***, showing that God's words carry power to restore health.

The apostles in the New Testament also demonstrated this authority. Peter and John healed a lame man at the gate called Beautiful by declaring, *"Silver and gold I do not have, but what I do have I give you: In the name of Jesus Christ of Nazareth, rise up and walk"* **(Acts 3:6).** Paul, too, commanded sickness and evil to leave in the name of Jesus, performing miracles through spoken words **(Acts 16:18).**

Even today, countless testimonies in the body of Christ show that God works through words. Every miracle, every act of deliverance, and every blessing begins with a declaration of faith in alignment with God's Word. Words are not just expressions; they are instruments of creation, authority, and life.

Practical Framework for Crafting Declarations

Declaring the Word of God in our lives is not something that happens automatically. For the first few months, believers need to make a deliberate effort to craft declarations in alignment with the Bible and take time to speak them daily. These declarations are not the same as positive affirmations. While affirmations are based on human optimism, biblical declarations are rooted in the promises of God. They carry divine authority because they are built on Scripture. Crafting and declaring Scripture-based words is a purposeful spiritual discipline. It requires intentional alignment with God's Word, daily practice, and spiritual discernment.

I once heard a preacher say that in these end times**, it is dangerous to begin the day without declaring the Word of God**. I fully agree with this. Jesus warned, *"But while men slept, his enemy came and sowed tares among the wheat and went his way"* **Matthew 13:25**. This reveals a spiritual truth: if we fail to sow the good seed of God's Word into our lives, the enemy will look for opportunities to sow negative seeds through circumstances, distractions, or influences. Declarations are not empty slogans. They are faith-filled, Scripture-based statements intentionally spoken to shape our reality in line with God's promises.

In my personal walk, I dedicate thirty minutes each day to speak declarations over my life. This practice began in 2020 during a seven-day fasting program at **Alleluia Ministries International**, under the leadership of my spiritual father. At that time, he gave us **'77 Declarations'**, and later **'90 Declarations'**, carefully written to cover every area of life. These were presented in video format, and I later added more to create a six-page document. This routine has helped me set the tone for each day. It fills me with confidence, reminding me that no matter the situation, I am called to rule and thrive.

Here are some guidelines for crafting declarations. Begin by searching the Scriptures for verses that have personal meaning or that speak directly to the situations you are facing. Focus on promises that reveal God's character, His love, and His intentions for His children. As **Bishop Stephan Aduya** says, *contextualize the Word by putting your name into it*. Adapt these verses into the present tense and first person, turning general truths into personal declarations of faith.

For example, Romans 8:37 says, *"Yet in all these things we are more than conquerors through Him who loved us."* This can be declared as: "I am more than a conqueror through Christ." Speak these declarations aloud daily, especially during morning devotionals or before facing challenges. Over time, repetition builds faith and confidence. Spiritual mentors and a church community can help nurture this practice.

Keep a written document or journal of your declarations, adding new ones as God reveals more promises to you in His Word. You can also record them in video or audio form to reinforce the habit. Unlike positive affirmations, biblical declarations draw strength from God's authority, not from human effort. They shift our focus to His power, provision, and goodness.

Here are a few sample declarations:

- I declare that He who raised Jesus Christ from the dead has already quickened and given life to my mortal body through the Holy Spirit (Romans

8:11). I speak refreshment and strength to my body in Jesus' name.

- I declare that I am under the blood of Jesus, and no weapon formed against me shall prosper. (Isaiah 54:17).
- I prophetically decree that my feet are catching speed and acceleration in the right direction. I will excel in everything I do, for the Lord is with me. (2 Samuel 5:10).
- I decree and declare that I am a child of God and an heir to the promises of God. (Romans 8:16–17).
- I declare that I am who God says I am, I have what God says I have, and I can do what God says I can do, in Jesus' name.
- In this month, I decree and declare that every promise of God made for me shall manifest, and every prophetic word spoken over my life will take form and shape, in Jesus' name. (2 Corinthians 1:20).

When declarations are spoken with faith, they plant seeds of life that shape the future, not immediately but definitely. From seed to shrub to an unshakable giant tree. They align our hearts, minds, and words with the will of God, bringing breakthrough, protection, and blessing into every area of life.

Chapter 7

Stewardship of Time and Talents

What is Stewardship?

Stewardship means being responsible for the time and abilities that God has given us. It is not about ownership, but about managing these gifts with care. Everything we have, including our time and our talents, belongs to God. We are called to use them wisely and for His glory. Stewardship is living each day as a gift from God, investing our hours and skills with gratitude, wisdom, and generosity so that everything we do becomes part of His greater plan.

The Bible gives us clear guidance about stewardship. In the beginning, Adam was placed in the Garden of Eden *"to tend and keep it"* **(Genesis 2:15)**. This shows that humanity was given the role of caretaker and not of owner. **Psalm 24:1** also reminds us, *"The earth is the Lord's, and all its fullness, the world and those who dwell therein"*. We are simply managers of what belongs to God, and one day we will give an account of how we have used what He entrusted to us.

One of the most important teachings on stewardship is found in the Parable of the Talents **(Matthew 25:14–30)**. In this parable, a master gives three servants different amounts of money, each according to their ability. Two of them used what they were given and increased it, and the master praised them for their faithfulness. But the third servant buried his talent in fear and returned it without increase. The master rebuked him for wasting the opportunity. This parable teaches us that stewardship is not about how much we are given but about how faithfully we use it. God expects us to be diligent and fruitful with the time and talents He has entrusted to us.

"Every good gift and every perfect gift is from above, and comes down from the Father of lights, with whom there is no variation or shadow of turning." ***James 1:17*** Stewardship also reminds us that God is the giver of every gift. Our time, our skills, our opportunities, and even our breath come from Him. As stewards, we are called to act on His behalf, not just for our own benefit. Every time we serve others, use our abilities to do good, or share the gospel, we are practicing faithful stewardship. By doing so, we show our gratitude to God and acknowledge that everything comes from Him.

True stewardship is more than just managing what we have. It also means setting priorities, making time for God, developing our talents, and finding a healthy balance between work and rest. Each day offers new opportunities to use what God has placed in our hands. If we do not use these opportunities, they may be lost.

Let us think of a simple story. Three friends—Smith, Grace, and John—were each given a blank notebook. The giver asked them to use it to record something meaningful each day. Smith wrote daily words of gratitude and kindness. Grace filled her notebook with creative ideas and solutions that helped her friends. But John put his notebook away, waiting for the perfect moment, and never used it. After a year, the giver came back. Smith and Grace presented notebooks full of growth and service, while John's notebook was empty. The chance to use it had quietly slipped away.

This story reminds us that stewardship is about how we choose to fill the days and opportunities God gives us. Every moment is a gift. When we use our time with kindness, our talents with creativity, and our lives with purpose, we honour God as faithful stewards.

The Gift and Value of Time

Time is one of the most precious gifts God has given us. It is both limited and divine. Every day we live is a day entrusted to us by the Lord, and each moment carries eternal value. James reminds us that our life is like *"a vapor that appears for a little time and then vanishes away"* **(James 4:14)**. This teaches us not to waste our days but to live with purpose and gratitude. **Psalm 139:16** says that all the days of our life are written in God's book before one of them comes to be. This truth shows that time is not random. It is planned by God, and we are called to use it with care and discipline.

The Bible encourages us to use time wisely and not to live carelessly. Paul writes, *"See then that you walk circumspectly, not as fools but as wise, redeeming the time, because the days are evil"* **(Ephesians 5:15–16)**. Redeeming the time means making the most of every opportunity God gives. Wasted hours are not just moments lost but missed opportunities to serve, love, grow, and glorify God. The Parable of the Talents **(Matthew 25:14–30)** can also be applied to time. Just as the servants were entrusted with different amounts and called to be faithful, so each of us is entrusted with a certain number of days and called to use them fruitfully.

Throughout Scripture we see men and women of God using their time and abilities wisely. Starting with our role model, **Jesus** rose early to pray, setting aside time for communion with the Father even when His ministry was demanding **(Mark 1:35)**. **Nehemiah** carefully planned and led the rebuilding of Jerusalem's wall in only fifty two days by staying focused and organizing the people **(Nehemiah 6:15)**. **The Virtuous Woman** described in Proverbs 31 used her time to balance work, care for her household, and service to others with diligence and foresight **(Proverbs 31:13–27). Paul** made the best use of every opportunity, tirelessly teaching, traveling, and encouraging the churches **(Acts 20:24). Moses** learned to delegate responsibilities to others so that his time could be spent on the most important tasks **(Exodus 18:24–26). Joseph** used years of abundance to prepare for famine, saving Egypt and surrounding nations through careful planning

(Genesis 41:46–57). These examples remind us that time is to be managed with wisdom, discipline, and purpose.

In the same way, believers today can practice wise stewardship of time. A young professional may set aside quiet time each morning for prayer and reflection, seeking God's guidance for daily decisions. Parents may choose to spend intentional evenings with their children, building love and unity at home rather than being consumed by endless work. A student may learn to avoid distractions, dedicating time to study and volunteering in meaningful service. Each of these choices reflects the principle of honoring God by using time for what matters most.

Wise stewardship of time is not simply about scheduling or productivity. It is about offering each day back to God as worship. When we are present in the moment, when we put our energy into what has eternal value, and when we align our choices with God's will, time becomes multiplied in its impact. Every hour then becomes an opportunity to glorify God, bless others, and grow in faith.

Principles of Time Stewardship

Time stewardship is about more than managing a calendar. It is about aligning daily life with God's purposes and living with intention. God has given each person the same twenty-four hours in a day, but how we use those hours determines whether our lives bear fruit for His kingdom or become consumed by distractions.

Stewardship of time means recognizing that every moment is a trust from God and learning to use it in ways that honour Him.

The first principle of time stewardship is setting God-centered priorities. Jesus said, *"But seek first the kingdom of God and His righteousness, and all these things shall be added to you"* **(Matthew 6:33)**. This means that spiritual growth, worship, and service to others should not be optional extras in life but the foundation of our schedules. When believers place God first, everything else falls into its proper place. For example, a manager may choose to begin her day with prayer and Scripture reading before reviewing her work tasks. If an unexpected assignment threatens to overshadow her time with family or her devotion to God, she pauses to remember her true priorities. In this way, she evaluates her schedule not only by urgency but by eternal value.

A second principle is the idea of a **"time budget."** Just as money must be budgeted carefully, time must be allocated wisely. Paul reminds us to walk *"circumspectly, not as fools but as wise, redeeming the time, because the days are evil"* **(Ephesians 5:15–16)**. This means choosing where our hours go before they slip away. A time budget involves setting aside blocks of time for different areas of life—work, family, rest, service, and spiritual growth. A student, for example, may plan his mornings for study, set aside Sundays for worship and community service, and keep his evenings free for rest and fellowship with friends and family. By making a plan, he avoids wasting time and reduces stress, while still leaving room for flexibility.

Another important principle is **balance**. Stewardship of time is not simply about doing more, but about living according to God's design. The Bible teaches the importance of work, but also of rest and relationships. God Himself rested on the seventh day after creation, establishing the principle of Sabbath **(Genesis 2:2–3).** Overworking leads to exhaustion and broken relationships, while underworking wastes opportunities. True balance comes from giving time to work, worship, rest, and community. For instance, a business-person may set clear boundaries on his work hours, schedule regular breaks for renewal, and devote evenings to family. By evaluating his schedule each week, he avoids burnout and lives in harmony with God's order.

Faithful time stewardship also requires learning to say "no." Not every opportunity is from God, and not every demand is necessary. Saying "no" to distractions creates room to say "yes" to prayer, service, meaningful work, and healthy relationships. This is not always easy, but it is necessary to protect what matters most. When believers centre their lives on God's purposes, their days become filled with peace, fruitfulness, and joy.

In today's world, social media and smartphones are like double-edged swords. They can provide unlimited information, useful tools, and meaningful connections. At the same time, they also bring endless distractions that can steal our focus and waste our time. If we do not discipline our use of them, they will end up controlling us. Large companies spend billions of dollars to keep people engaged on their apps. They even hire psychologists to study human behaviour, using that knowledge—originally meant to help people grow and reach their potential—as a weapon against our attention.

This is why it is wise to set boundaries. Uninstall unnecessary apps, turn off notifications, use restricted modes, and keep your phone on silent or switched off when working or spending time with loved ones. By taking these simple steps, you protect your focus, guard your relationships, and honour God with your time.

In the end, time stewardship is not about controlling every moment but about surrendering our moments to God. Each day offers chances to grow in faith, bless others, and live purposefully. When time is managed with God at the centre, life becomes balanced, relationships flourish, and every hour reflects His greater plan.

Challenges and Solutions in Managing Time

Managing time is one of the greatest struggles of modern life. While every person receives the same number of hours in a day, many find their days slipping away without fruitfulness. The Bible reminds us to "redeem the time, because the days are evil" **(Ephesians 5:16)**. This means we must be intentional in overcoming distractions and misuses of time.

One common challenge is **procrastination**. Many people delay important tasks until the last minute, which often creates stress and missed deadlines. Instead of using time wisely, hours are wasted in avoidance. **Proverbs 20:4** says, *"The lazy man will not plow* *because of winter; he will beg during harvest and have nothing".* Procrastination robs both peace and productivity.

Another challenge is **multitasking.** Trying to do many things at once may seem productive, but it usually reduces focus and quality. Tasks take longer, and mistakes increase. Jesus said, *"No one can serve two masters"* **(Matthew 6:24).** This principle also applies to our attention. Divided focus weakens results, while single-minded effort brings clarity and excellence.

The frequent use of **social media and smartphones** is another major distraction. Constant notifications break concentration and steal valuable time. Hours spent scrolling often leave people empty rather than refreshed. **Psalm 90:12** teaches, *"So teach us to number our days, that we may gain a heart of wisdom".* Wise time management requires discipline in using technology.

Overcommitment is a common issue. Many people take on too many responsibilities out of fear of missing out or disappointing others. Out of kindness or fear of conflict, people accept more tasks than they can realistically handle. This leads to stress and reduced effectiveness. Clear communication and honest limits honour God and protect time.

This often leads to exhaustion and inefficiency. Even Jesus, though surrounded by many needs, sometimes withdrew from the crowds to pray and rest (Luke 5:16). Once, **Dad Alph** shared about a person who sought help for a habit of lying. In response, God revealed that the root issue was overcommitment. Simply addressing this habit created room for improvement. Learning to say "no" allows space for renewal and helps us focus on God's priorities.

Interruptions can also derail productivity. Constant phone calls, emails, or conversations break concentration and force people to restart tasks repeatedly. Without boundaries, small interruptions consume large amounts of time. Guarding focus becomes essential for faithful stewardship.

Finally, **a lack of clear priorities** leaves many living reactively rather than intentionally. When all tasks seem equally urgent, people jump from task to task without real progress. Without vision, energy is wasted. **Proverbs 29:18** says, *"Where there is no revelation, the people cast off restraint"*. A clear plan rooted in God's purposes gives direction and focus.

Thankfully, God provides wisdom for overcoming these challenges. Practical tools and faithful habits can transform the way time is managed. **Scheduling** and **time blocking** is one such tool. By dividing the day into focused periods for work, family, spiritual growth, and rest, people can live with balance. This ensures that no important area of life is neglected.

Another helpful practice is **setting boundaries**. Establishing "do not disturb" times limits interruptions and creates space for deep focus. For example, switching phones to silent during prayer or family meals protects what matters most. Boundaries reflect the biblical principle of guarding the heart: *"Keep your heart with all diligence, for out of it spring the issues of life"* **(Proverbs 4:23)**.

Reflection periods are also powerful. Taking a few minutes each day or a longer pause each week to evaluate how time has been spent allows for correction and renewal. Honest reflection helps believers realign their schedule with God's will.

To-do lists and prioritization are another simple but effective tools. Writing down what needs to be done clarifies responsibilities and keeps the mind from being overwhelmed. By identifying which tasks matter most, believers can avoid wasting time on trivial matters and give their best to what counts.

Technology itself, though often a distraction, can also be used wisely. Apps that track time, set reminders, or block social media can support discipline and focus. When used with self-control, these tools can help people redeem their hours for meaningful purposes.

Delegation is also essential. Moses learned this lesson when Jethro advised him to appoint leaders to share responsibilities so he would not wear himself out **(Exodus 18:24–26).** Sharing tasks with others not only prevents burnout but also empowers others to grow in their own gifts.

As discussed erlier, One practical technique for focus is the **Pomodoro Technique.** This method divides work into short sessions of twenty-five minutes, called "pomodoros," followed by a five-minute break. After four sessions, a longer break is taken. These short, focused intervals train the mind to resist distractions and maintain energy. The regular breaks prevent burnout and make large tasks feel manageable. By reviewing progress after each cycle, individuals also learn to adjust their workflow for greater effectiveness. This simple rhythm can transform long, tiring workdays into fruitful ones.

Time management will always face challenges, but with God's wisdom and practical discipline, believers can overcome them. By setting priorities, creating boundaries, reflecting often, and using tools wisely, time becomes not a burden but a blessing. Faithful stewardship allows every hour to be offered to God, leading to peace, productivity, and purpose.

The Nature and Source of Talents

Talents are special gifts from God that reflect His unique design and purpose for every individual. These talents include both natural abilities and spiritual gifts. Natural talents are often inherited through family, culture, and training, while spiritual gifts are imparted directly by the Holy Spirit to believers in Christ. Together, these make up the abilities we are called to steward for the glory of God and the service of others. The Bible reminds us in **James 1:17**, *"Every good gift and every perfect gift is from above, and comes down from the Father of lights, with whom there is no variation or shadow of turning."*

Natural talents are those skills and aptitudes people are either born with or develop through experience and practice. For example, some may have artistic ability, musical talent, leadership qualities, or teaching skills. These gifts are not limited to believers; they are present in all people because God has created each person with a unique purpose. These talents can be sharpened and expanded through discipline and dedication, and when directed toward God's glory, they become powerful tools for blessing others.

Spiritual gifts, on the other hand, are given specifically to believers by the Holy Spirit when they come to faith in Christ. These are not simply natural skills but divine empowerments for ministry and service. Paul explains in **1 Corinthians 12:7**, *"But the manifestation of the Spirit is given to each one for the profit of all."* Spiritual gifts may include prophecy, healing, teaching, leadership, and many others (Romans 12:3-8; 1 Corinthians 12:8-11; Ephesians 4:11-12). Unlike natural talents that may benefit personal success, spiritual gifts are entrusted for the building up of the church and the advancement of God's kingdom.

Both natural talents and spiritual gifts are never meant for selfish gain. They are entrusted to us so that through them God may be glorified, and others may be blessed. As Peter wrote in **1 Peter 4:10**, *"As each one has received a gift, minister it to one another, as good stewards of the manifold grace of God."* Talents can be refined through learning and practice, while spiritual gifts often grow and reveal themselves more clearly over time as a believer matures in faith and obedience.

Discovering and Identifying Talents

Recognizing the talents God has placed within us is an important step toward faithful stewardship. Discovering them involves reflection, seeking feedback from others, and prayerful discernment.

Reflection allows us to examine the activities that bring joy, fulfilment, and consistent fruit. Talents are often connected to passions and areas where we feel alive and capable. If certain activities repeatedly bring satisfaction and success, they may point to God-given talents that need to be developed further.

Feedback from others also plays a significant role. Sometimes we overlook the abilities that come naturally to us, but others can clearly see them. Friends, mentors, or church leaders can affirm and confirm the gifts and strengths we might not recognize ourselves. **Proverbs 27:17** says, *"As iron sharpens iron, so a man sharpens the countenance of his friend."* Honest encouragement and counsel help us discover and refine our abilities.

Spiritual discernment is essential in identifying gifts that are divinely given by the Spirit. Prayer, listening to God's voice, and seeking guidance from Scripture bring clarity to how God has equipped us. In addition, observing the doors of opportunity God opens in our lives can help confirm how He intends us to use these talents.

Experimentation also helps in the process of discovery. By trying different areas of service or ministry, we can sense where our talents and spiritual gifts fit best. Some gifts only become clear when we actively step out in faith and serve in new ways.

Finally, **biblical understanding** provides a foundation for recognizing talents and gifts. Scripture teaches us that all gifts are given for the common good and for the building up of the body of Christ. This truth reminds us that both natural talents and spiritual gifts are not for pride or personal gain, but to glorify God and serve others in love.

In summary, talents are God-given abilities, both natural and spiritual. Natural talents may be inherited or developed, while spiritual gifts are imparted by the Holy Spirit. Discovering them requires self-reflection, guidance from others, and spiritual discernment. When identified and faithfully used, these talents become instruments of service that bless others, strengthen the church, and fulfil God's purposes in our lives.

Developing and Using Talents Faithfully

Talents, whether natural abilities or spiritual gifts, are responsibilities from God. They are not given to us by accident but are entrusted for a purpose. Just as the master in the Parable of the Talents entrusted his servants with resources to manage wisely **(Matthew 25:14–30)**, God expects us to nurture and multiply the talents He has placed in our lives. Developing these talents requires intentional effort, faith, and obedience.

The first step is **self-discovery and evaluation**. We must take time to identify our strengths and weaknesses. This comes through personal reflection and by listening to the counsel of others who can help us see what we might overlook. **Proverbs 20:5** reminds us, *"Counsel in the heart of man is like deep water, but a man of understanding will draw it out."* Honest evaluation enables us to know where growth is needed and how we can best serve God.

Next is **learning and practice**. Talents grow when we actively invest in them. This means studying, training, and practicing regularly. Just as a musician improves by rehearsing daily or a teacher sharpens their ability by studying, we also must put effort into developing our God-given talents. **Proverbs 22:29** says, *"Do you see a man who excels in his work? He will stand before kings; he will not stand before unknown men."* Excellence comes only through discipline and perseverance.

Another key is **faith and perseverance**. Developing talents is not always easy. At times we may feel discouraged or face obstacles, but we must trust God's help and continue pressing forward. **Philippians 4:13** declares, *"I can do all things through Christ who strengthens me."* With faith and persistence, weaknesses can be transformed into strengths, and talents can be used far beyond what we imagine.

Finally, we need **courage to use talents**. Fear of failure, criticism, or comparison often holds people back from using their gifts. Yet, hiding our abilities dishonours God. When we step out in courage, we show faith in the One who gave us those talents. As Jesus said in **Matthew 25:29**, *"For to everyone who has, more will be given, and he will have abundance; but from him who does not have, even what he has will be taken away."* Faithful use leads to multiplication and blessing.

Applying Talents in Service

Talents find their true purpose when they are used to serve God and others. They are not meant for self-centred pursuits but for advancing God's kingdom and being a blessing in every sphere of life.

One way talents are applied is **serving the church**. The body of Christ needs the diverse gifts of its members to grow strong. Teaching, preaching, worship, leadership, hospitality, or encouragement are all valuable in strengthening believers. As **Ephesians 4:12** teaches, gifts are given *"for the equipping of the saints for the work of ministry, for the edifying of the body of Christ."*

Talents also make a difference in **community impact**. Using our skills outside the church to meet needs in society shows the love of Christ in practical ways. A doctor, teacher, businessperson, or artist can reflect God's character through their work and service, bringing light to their community. **Matthew 5:16** reminds us, *"Let your light so shine before men, that they may see your good works and glorify your Father in heaven."*

In addition, talents shape our **everyday influence**. We can use our abilities in family life, workplaces, and friendships. These settings give opportunities to encourage, inspire, and witness for Christ through both words and actions. Even the simplest act of using our gifts in daily life can become a testimony of God's grace.

All of this requires **faithful stewardship**. Talents are not to be hoarded for personal gain or pride but entrusted for God's purposes. **1 Peter 4:10** reminds us, *"As each one has received a gift, minister it to one another, as good stewards of the manifold grace of God."* Faithful stewardship means prayerfully seeking God's guidance on where and how to apply our gifts.

Avoiding Neglect and Misuse of Talents

The Bible warns about neglecting or misusing talents. In the Parable of the Talents, the servant who hid his gift in the ground out of fear and laziness was called *"wicked and lazy"* **(Matthew 25:26)**. This shows that ignoring or misusing what God has given us is a serious matter.

Hiding talents often comes from fear, doubt, or a lack of confidence. When we refuse to use our gifts, we miss opportunities for growth and blessing. Fear should never stop us from obeying God's call.

Misusing talents for selfish gain is another danger. When abilities are directed toward pride, ambition, or ungodly purposes, they no longer glorify God. Instead, they harm others and rob us of the joy of true service. For example, Balaam, a pagan prophet, was once restrained by God from cursing Israel and was made to bless them instead. Later, however, he advised the Midianites on how to lead Israel into idolatry and immorality, which turned God's favor away from them. Eventually, Balaam himself was killed in battle.

Ignoring opportunities can also lead to wasted potential. Distractions, excuses, or misplaced priorities cause many to set aside their talents. As a result, they miss out on the fruitfulness God intended. Scripture teaches that God holds us accountable for how we use our gifts.

Finally, there are **spiritual consequences** for neglecting or misusing talents. God expects us to bear fruit. Unfaithfulness results in loss of stewardship and blessing. Yet there is also encouragement. **Romans**

11:29 tells *"For the gifts and the calling of God are irrevocable."* If we have neglected or misused talents in the past, God's grace is available. Through repentance and renewed commitment, He restores us and empowers us to grow again.

Faithfully developing and using talents involves purposeful growth, courageous application, and careful stewardship. We must avoid neglect or misuse, remembering that every gift is entrusted by God. When we nurture our talents and use them in service to others, we honour God and bless the world. In doing so, we live as faithful stewards who will one day hear the words, *"Well done, good and faithful servant"* **(Matthew 25:21).**

Accountability and Eternal Perspective

The Bible teaches that God is the true owner of everything, including our time and talents. We are not independent owners but stewards who will one day give an account of how we managed what was entrusted to us. This truth gives weight and seriousness to the way we live each day. **Romans 14:12** says, *"So then each of us shall give account of himself to God."* This verse reminds us that no one is exempt from accountability. Each person will stand before the Lord and answer for how they used their resources, opportunities, and abilities.

The Parable of the Talents in **Matthew 25:14–30** provides a vivid picture of this accountability. In the story, the master entrusted his servants with different amounts of talents before leaving. Upon his return, he evaluated each servant based on their faithfulness. Those who invested and multiplied their talents were rewarded, but the one who hid his talent out of fear was rebuked and punished. This parable teaches that stewardship is not passive. God expects us to use what He has given us with diligence, courage, and purpose. Wasting or hiding our gifts shows unfaithfulness to His trust.

Accountability also shapes how believers live daily. It calls us to **intentional living** instead of drifting through life carelessly. Every hour and every skill matter because God has given them for a reason. Stewardship means making choices that reflect God's will and priorities rather than our own convenience or comfort. Knowing that God will examine how we used our time and talents should encourage us to walk in wisdom and faithfulness.

Faithful stewardship is not only about responsibility but also about reward. Jesus described how the faithful servants in the parable received both praise and greater responsibility. The master told them, *"Well done, good and faithful servant... Enter into the joy of your lord"* **(Matthew 25:21)**. This shows that stewardship brings not only earthly fruitfulness but also eternal joy and reward in God's presence.

The apostle Paul also gave encouragement about eternal motivation. In **Colossians 3:23–24**, he wrote, *"And whatever you do, do it heartily, as to the Lord and not to men, knowing that from the Lord you will receive the reward of the inheritance; for you serve the Lord Christ."* This perspective lifts ordinary work into eternal significance. Every act of faithfulness, whether great or small, done unto the Lord will be remembered and rewarded.

Paul also reminds believers in **2 Corinthians 5:10**, *"For we must all appear before the judgment seat of Christ, that each one may receive the things done in the body, according to what he has done, whether good or bad."* This sober truth motivates us to live with holiness and integrity, knowing that every choice has eternal weight.

In summary, accountability to God compels us to steward our time and talents wisely. The promise of eternal reward inspires us to stay faithful even when the work is difficult or unnoticed by others. With this eternal perspective, believers can live with purpose, seeking not temporary gains but the lasting joy of glorifying God and building His kingdom.

Chapter 8

Community and Accountability

We were never created to face life's battles alone. God designed us to grow through relationships that strengthen, guide, and support us. Community is His gift—a place where we are encouraged when weak, corrected when needed, and celebrated when victorious. In a world that praises independence, Scripture reminds us that true strength is found in walking together. This chapter explores why community matters, how it shapes our spiritual growth, and how accountability helps us live as more than conquerors.

The Biblical Basis for Community

When God said, *"It is not good for the man to be alone"* **(Genesis 2:18)**, He was revealing a truth about all people—not just about marriage. God created us with a deep need for relationships. We are designed to grow, learn, and be strengthened through others. In **Acts**

2:42–47, we see the early believers living this out. They devoted themselves to teaching, fellowship, sharing meals, and praying together. Their community was not just a meeting; it was a way of life. They supported one another with generosity, love, and shared faith. This shows that real biblical fellowship is both spiritual and practical. It involves giving, sharing, caring, and reflecting God's relational heart.

Paul also describes the Church as the **Body of Christ**, where every member has a unique and important role. Just like the human body needs every organ to function well, the Church needs every believer to use their gifts. No part is unnecessary, and no believer is meant to live independently. This picture teaches us unity in diversity—we are different, but we need each other. Community is the place where God's grace flows through each person to strengthen the whole body.

The book of Ecclesiastes teaches the same truth: "*Two are better than one.*" Companionship multiplies strength. When one person falls, the other can help them stand again. A companion brings comfort in difficult seasons and protection in times of danger. Spiritually, this is the foundation of accountability. An accountability partner helps you stay strong during setbacks, failures, and discouragement. Community ensures that no believer fights alone; each one is supported, encouraged, and reminded of God's promises when their faith becomes weak.

Hebrews reminds us to "spur one another on

toward love and good deeds" and not to give up meeting together. This instruction is not only about attending church services—it is about living in fellowship and building each other up. True community challenges us when we become complacent, nurtures compassion in our hearts, and strengthens our perseverance. It turns isolated faith into shared faith and personal strength into collective strength. For example, when you fail an interview or exam and share it with a spiritually mature believer, their insight from God's Word can open your eyes to the unseen spiritual truths. Their encouragement and correction help you see the situation not as failure but as preparation. Your perspective changes, and with new hope, you choose to rise again.

Jesus Himself modeled the importance of community. He did not carry out His ministry alone. He chose twelve disciples to walk with Him. He taught them through conversations, meals, travel, and everyday experiences. This was not random friendship—it was intentional mentorship and accountability. Within the twelve, Jesus formed an even closer relationship with Peter, James, and John. This shows that deeper spiritual growth often happens in small, trusted circles. Jesus invited His disciples into His mission and even into His moments of struggle, showing us how real community functions.

The early Church continued this pattern. In the book of Acts, we see believers sharing their possessions, supporting each other during persecution, and praying together with unity and passion. When one person suffered, the whole community felt the pain. When one person rejoiced, the others shared the joy. Their unity and love were so strong that outsiders were drawn to them. Their fellowship glorified God and strengthened their faith. Their example invites us today to rediscover the power of shared purpose and spiritual accountability—an environment where faith grows stronger through connection and commitment.

The Power of Encouragement and Support

Encouragement is one of the strongest spiritual tools God has given His people. A single faith-filled word can lift a discouraged heart, renew strength, and bring light into a dark moment. The Bible shows that encouragement is not just emotional comfort—it is an act of love and obedience. When believers speak life to one another, they reflect the heart of Christ, who restored people, inspired them, and gave them the courage to continue.

Hebrews 10:24–25 teaches us to think about how we can *"stir up one another to love and good works."* This means encouragement should be intentional and active. It is more than saying something nice; it is helping someone move toward victory—whether in faith, work, studies, or personal battles. During seasons of doubt, delay, or disappointment, a timely encouraging word can reignite purpose. In the Christian journey, growth often happens through the prayers, support, and compassion of people who genuinely want us to succeed.

Daniel and his three friends—Shadrach, Meshach, and Abednego—show the strength of godly support. Living in Babylon, they were surrounded by ungodly influences, yet their unity helped them stay faithful. **Daniel 1:8** says he *"purposed in his heart" not to defile himself with the king's food.* If he were alone, he might have compromised. But because they stood together, their shared courage helped them remain strong. Their story teaches that encouragement among godly friends builds endurance and keeps convictions firm even in hostile environments.

God never intended His children to carry guilt or burdens alone. **James 5:16** encourages believers to *"confess your trespasses to one another, and pray for one another, that you may be healed."* Honesty brings healing. When believers open their hearts in a safe and loving community, shame loses its power and restoration begins.

Paul also wrote, *"Bear one another's burdens, and so fulfil the law of Christ"* **Galatians 6:2.** True support is not just feeling sorry for someone—it is compassion expressed through action. It is praying, helping, listening, and standing with someone in their struggles. This kind of support builds trust, deepens relationships, and creates emotional and spiritual health.

Isolation weakens faith, but community builds it. Our words, guided by the Holy Spirit, have creative power. **Proverbs 18:21** says, "*Death and life are in the power of the tongue.*" Speaking life means declaring God's truth, reminding others of His promises, and strengthening their faith when fear tries to take over. Encouraging words can change the atmosphere of a home, a church, or even a troubled heart.

In contrast, isolation allows doubts, negative thoughts, and fear to grow unchecked. The enemy often uses loneliness to weaken believers. But when we speak grace, hope, and Scripture to one another, we replace despair with joy and confusion with clarity.

Personal testimonies are also powerful tools of encouragement. **Revelation 12:11** says "*And they overcame him by the blood of the Lamb and by the word of their testimony...*" When we share stories of answered prayer, healing, provision, or breakthroughs, it strengthens the faith of others. Testimonies remind us that what God has done before, He can do again. They create hope, build expectation, and show that perseverance is rewarded. Every believer's testimony becomes a message that inspires someone else to stand firm.

Paul's command in **1 Thessalonians 5:11** – "*Therefore comfort each other and edify one another, just as you also are doing.*" – teaches that encouragement is a daily ministry. Faith grows stronger in environments filled with declaration and support.

Encouragement reminds weary believers that their efforts matter and that God is still working even when results are not visible. It fuels perseverance and helps people keep moving forward with renewed confidence.

Openness also plays a key role in genuine fellowship. When Christians share their struggles—not just their victories—it allows grace to flow more freely. Jesus said, "Where two or three gather in My name, there am I in the midst of them." United prayer brings multiplied power. It strengthens relationships, deepens trust, and brings healing to hearts.

In a world where many hide pain behind smiles, Godly community creates space for honesty and compassion. Whether through prayer groups, testimony videos, a Christ-centered social media group or simple one-on-one conversations, believers grow stronger when they carry one another's burdens and celebrate one another's victories. Such support turns a church or fellowship into a spiritual family marked by love, hope, and endurance.

Therefore, surround yourself with people like this, and also become a person like this for others. Receive support, encouragement, and practical guidance and also be someone who gives support, shares solutions, and stands with others in their struggles.

Types of Accountabilities

Accountability is not a restriction or a burden. It is a protective covering that God designed to help believers grow, stay focused, and walk faithfully in every area of life. When we understand it the right way, accountability becomes a blessing that guards our calling, strengthens our character, and keeps us on the path God has set for us. God uses relationships, guidance, and community to help His people move from potential failure to maturity, from confusion to clarity, and from isolation to growth.

Every believer is accountable to God. He/She must first learn to take responsibility for their own life before God. **Romans 14:12** says, *"Each of us will give an account of ourselves to God."* We will not be judged but we will have to give account, it reminds us that our time, talents, and opportunities matter. **Personal accountability** means living with the awareness that God sees every choice we make. A healthy life includes moments of honest self-reflection. Through prayer evaluating our actions, we see areas that need correction, discipline, or redirection. This helps us develop our everyday life. Personal accountability is not meant to create guilt or regret but it is meant to create growth-oriented changes.

The second type of accountability is with **accountability partners**. No one matures alone. **Proverbs 27:17** teaches, *"As iron sharpens iron, so one person sharpens another."* Accountability partners help us stay focused, persistent and growing. These relationships are built on trust and prayer. Partners encourage us, correct us when needed, and help us stay committed to our goals. They are usually one or two people who walk closely with us. Just as iron becomes sharper through contact, believers grow stronger through honest conversations and solution-filled healthy correction or feedback. This type of accountability protects us from compromise and builds resilience in moments of disappointments.

The early Church showed the power of small groups **(Acts 2:46)**. They met in homes, prayed, shared meals, and learned together. These small gatherings created safe places where people could share struggles and victories openly. In our ministry, we call them "**cells.**" Our leader often says, "*We are not a church that only gathers on Sundays; we are a church made of everyday cells.*" Today, physical distance is not a barrier. A WhatsApp group or an online community of 30–50 students or professionals can become a place for growth. Just as hobby groups help guitarists or athletes grow together, small groups of Christ-centered believers help to develop each other in both faith and life. These communities turn Christianity from a weekly activity into daily participation, no matter where they work.

Another type is '**Mentorship'.** Throughout the Bible, mentorship is essential for growth. Paul mentored Timothy by guiding, correcting, and equipping him for ministry. Moses mentored Joshua, and Elijah mentored

Elisha—passing wisdom, courage, and spiritual strength from one generation to the next. Mentorship strengthens both the mentor and the student. It multiplies growth, deepens purpose, and creates strong foundations for the future. There are so many people in every field to teach the young generation the things that took years of trial and error. Take up online courses, books, personal tutors or any digital way to learn something new in your field. Join week-end classes to upgrade your skillset. Without continuous learning, you may become outdated soon because AI is replacing humans and the fast changing world demands continuous growth.

Peer accountability also plays a powerful role. It happens among equals—friends, coworkers, partners, or worship teams. These relationships are built on mutual support and shared goals. They help each person stay consistent, overcome setbacks, and celebrate progress. For example, a girl gifted in singing may need others in upscaling her singing like someone to write lyrics, someone to play instruments, and someone to coach her voice. Together, they help her grow. Peer accountability reminds us that growth is not a solo journey—it is a shared pursuit where love and truth work together.

Finally, **Spiritual accountability** provides spiritual covering. God appoints leaders to guide His people **(Hebrews 13:17)** and church authority ordains leaders over people. Spiritual oversight is not about control but care. Leaders help believers make wise choices, offer correction when needed, and give counsel based on Scripture and real-life understanding. Submitting to godly leadership cultivates humility and safety. When people open their lives to wise leaders, they protect themselves from deception and drifting away. Strong, Bible-based leadership provides teaching, healing, and restoration, helping believers grow spiritually & emotionally which eventually help them to grow professionally.

All these forms of accountability—personal, relational, and communal—work together like a safety net. Each believer grows best when they combine personal devotion, honest friendships, wise mentors, and spiritual leadership. Together, these create a supportive environment where holiness, character, and faith can flourish.

In God's Kingdom, accountability is rooted in love—not fear. It exists to build trust, develop discipline, and strengthen perseverance. When believers walk in mutual accountability, they protect each other, grow together, and reflect the unity and purity of the Body of Christ.

Practical Steps to Build Godly Relationships

God created people to grow through relationships. Whether at home, school, work, or church, the people around us shape our thinking, our decisions, and our spiritual health. The right relationships push us toward our purpose, while the wrong ones quietly pull us away from it. Building godly relationships requires intentional choices, spiritual discernment, and daily grace. It means surrounding ourselves with people who strengthen our faith, sharpen our character, and encourage us to live out biblical values consistently.

The Bible teaches, "*Do not be unequally yoked with unbelievers*" **2 Corinthians 6:14**. This doesn't mean we reject everyone who believes differently; it means we choose our closest relationships wisely. In school, college, or the workplace, we can interact with many people while still being careful about who speaks into our life. Like-minded companions share our values and help us stay grounded. These are friends or coworkers who uplift our faith, respect our convictions, and support our God-given dreams. Building such relationships does not happen by chance—pray for God to bring people who will speak truth with love and walk with you through victories and struggles.

Finding a mentor or accountability partner is an important step in spiritual and personal growth. Everyone needs guidance, whether they are a student making decisions, a professional handling challenges, or a parent managing responsibilities. A mentor is someone with more experience—someone who walks ahead of you in wisdom and faith. They guide you, correct you when needed, and encourage you with lessons from their own journey. Look for people who live consistently according to Scripture—pastors, teachers, relatives, or even coworkers with strong integrity. Approach them honestly and share your desire to grow. Accountability partners, on the other hand, are often peers who share similar goals. They pray with you, challenge your discipline, and help you stay committed to spiritual and practical habits. Together, you both grow stronger.

A godly relationship is marked by truth, humility, and consistency. Seek people who value honesty more than comfort—those who tell you the truth in love instead of saying what you want to hear. Look for those who respect your boundaries, protect your privacy, and celebrate your progress without jealousy. Good relationships strengthen your walk with God. They pray before advising, encourage you to stay faithful, and believe in your potential even when you feel discouraged.

Many people avoid opening up because of past hurts or betrayals. But genuine growth requires some level of vulnerability. Vulnerability is not weakness—it is courage. It means stepping out of your comfort zone to share your struggles, admit mistakes, or ask for prayer. A guarded heart may feel safe, but it remains stuck; an open heart grows, heals, and flourishes through healthy connection.

However, vulnerability must be guided by wisdom. **Proverbs 4:23** says, "*Guard your heart, for everything you do flows from it.*" Not everyone should have access to your deepest struggles. **Discernment** helps you identify trustworthy people—those who are consistent, spiritually grounded, and genuinely loving. Before sharing personal matters, observe how a person treats others. Someone who gossips about others will eventually gossip about you. A trustworthy person listens with compassion, keeps confidence, and offers counsel rooted in Scripture.

Even the best relationships require care and maintenance. Unity does not mean never disagreeing; it means staying anchored in love and forgiveness when conflict arises. Address problems early, speak respectfully, and pray before reacting. Do not "enable" unhealthy behavior in the name of kindness. True love restores, corrects, and protects. Establishing healthy boundaries helps relationships remain balanced. *Boundaries are not walls—they are gates that protect peace and allow love to grow in a healthy way.*

Boundaries are biblical. Even Jesus withdrew from crowds to rest and pray. In daily life, boundaries may look like saying "no" when you are overwhelmed, respecting others' time, or refusing to participate in activities that dishonor God. Healthy boundaries prevent emotional exhaustion and protect trust.

If you want to grow in discipline and consistency, forming an accountability partnership is powerful. Choose someone who shares your faith and values. Decide together how often to meet—weekly or biweekly—to pray, discuss your progress, and review your goals. These meetings become life-shaping sessions when done intentionally. You sharpen each other, encourage each other, and push each other toward spiritual and personal growth.

Every strong relationship depends on **healthy communication**. Speak gently, listen patiently, and respond with grace. **Colossians 4:6** teaches, "*Let your speech always be with grace.*" Whether at work, home, or school, respectful communication opens hearts and maintains peace. Practice active listening—focus fully, avoid assumptions, and honor the other person's perspective. Christlike communication transforms ordinary relationships into meaningful and life-giving ones.

When accountability is rooted in God's Word, it produces lasting transformation. People become more consistent, relationships grow healthier, and faith becomes stronger. Accountability never restricts you—it frees you to live with integrity, purpose, and joy.

Stories of real transformation often begin with relationships. A student who joins a prayer circle finds courage to resist peer pressure. A business leader who enters a Bible-based mentorship group begins to make better decisions. A couple in a small fellowship experiences healing through shared prayer and support. God uses relationships to shape destiny. Mentors, accountability partners, and faith communities help believers align their decisions with biblical principles—turning belief into daily practice and spiritual truths into real-life change.

Serving Others and Mutual Edification

Winning in life is not only about achieving your own goals—it is also about helping others succeed. True fulfillment comes when we learn to serve. Serving is not an optional activity in the Christian life; it is the very center of it. Every place—our homes, schools, workplaces, and communities—becomes healthier when people choose service over selfishness. Jesus taught that greatness in God's Kingdom comes through serving, not through status or position **(Mark 10:43–45)**. When we serve with love, we display the character of Christ and become channels of His grace in everyday situations.

Paul teaches, "*Serve one another humbly in love*" - **Galatians 5:13**. Service that pleases God comes from the heart, not from duty or pressure. In daily life, this might look like tutoring a classmate who feels lost, helping a coworker finish an urgent task, or supporting a family member during a difficult time. These simple acts may seem small, but when done in love, they carry eternal value. Loving service meets needs, but it also touches hearts. At work, it might mean showing understanding to someone under stress. At school or college, it could mean encouraging a friend who feels discouraged. In the home, it includes choosing patience, forgiving quickly, and helping joyfully. Service turns ordinary moments into opportunities for ministry.

Galatians 6:2 urges believers to "*carry each other's burdens.*" Life becomes easier when we share both struggles and victories. In a world where many feel alone, offering support—whether emotional, spiritual, or practical—brings healing to both the giver and the receiver. In practical terms, mutual support looks like coworkers helping instead of competing, students forming study groups to lift each other up, or families stepping in when someone needs extra care. Service builds compassion and unity. When believers serve together, the impact multiplies, and God's love becomes visible in powerful ways.

Every believer has been uniquely gifted by God. **Romans 12:4–8** compares the Church to a body with different parts, each one essential. Some people are gifted with encouragement, others with teaching, leadership, generosity, or mercy. These gifts are not meant to be used once a week—they are meant to be part of daily life. A teacher can share hope with students. A business leader can build ethical and fair workplaces. A homemaker can offer warmth and hospitality that refreshes others. When everyone uses the gifts God has given them, the community becomes stronger and more complete. In God's Kingdom, personal growth is not self-centered—it is about becoming the best version of yourself so you can serve others better. True success lifts others as it lifts you.

Paul also teaches that the strong should support the weak and work for their good **(Romans 15:1–2)**. This goes against the world's culture of self-promotion. Building others requires humility and the desire to help others succeed, even if you don't receive recognition. At school, this means helping a classmate who struggles instead of judging them. At work, it may involve mentoring a junior colleague or celebrating others' achievements. In families, edification happens through affirming words—speaking life, appreciation, and hope instead of criticism. Words that build create strength. Acts that uplift create courage. Together they produce an atmosphere where growth becomes natural.

When believers serve with love and unity, their lives become a light that points people to God. Jesus said His followers are *"the light of the world"* **(Matthew 5:14–16)**. This light shines not only through big acts but through everyday kindness, integrity, and compassion. Service transforms the one who receives it, but it also transforms the one who gives it. It teaches humility, expands empathy, and deepens spiritual maturity. Serving in church ministries, volunteering in the community, or simply helping neighbors strengthens gratitude and brings us closer to God's heart.

Communities built on service become places where faith naturally grows. People begin to notice the difference God makes in everyday life—workplaces become more peaceful, families become more supportive, and students become more encouraging. Mutual edification creates a culture where everyone rises together. Service is God's strategy for success—it develops the giver, blesses the receiver, and brings glory to God. Every act of service is not a loss of time or effort;

it is an investment into eternity.

The Dangers of Isolation and Wrong Associations

Success in life is shaped not only by hard work or intelligence but also by the relationships we choose. The people we allow close to us influence our thoughts, our decisions, and even our future. The Bible gives both encouragement and warning: godly relationships lead to wisdom and growth, while wrong influences can slowly pull us away from God's purpose. At the same time, isolating ourselves completely steals the support and accountability we need to grow. To succeed at home, school, work, and in spiritual life, we must choose our relationships carefully and avoid the trap of isolation.

Paul's warning is very clear: "*Do not be misled: Bad company corrupts good character.*" **(1 Corinthians 15:33)**. The people around us impact our values and behavior. Even a strong believer can slowly change if constantly surrounded by people who mock, ignore, or oppose godly principles. This can happen in friendships that normalize gossip, workplaces that encourage compromise, or social groups that pressure you into unhealthy habits. Wrong company does not always appear harmful—it may come disguised as charm, talent, or shared interests. But over time, it influences your speech, your lifestyle, and your priorities. Protecting your character means choosing relationships that help you grow, not ones that weaken your faith or lead you toward regret.

The Bible gives strong examples of people who failed because of wrong associations. **Samson** was chosen by God to deliver Israel, yet he lost his strength and purpose because he connected himself with people who did not respect his calling. His relationship with Delilah blinded him until it destroyed everything God gave him. This shows that emotional attraction or convenience should never replace spiritual wisdom in relationships—whether friendship, relationship /marriage, or work.

King Solomon also began with great wisdom, favor, and potential. But his relationships with foreign women led him into idolatry and spiritual decline **(1 Kings 11:1–4)**. Even the wisest person can fall when surrounded by wrong influences. Both Samson and Solomon show that wrong associations destroy purpose faster than any enemy from outside. Compromise usually begins small and ends in major spiritual loss. In everyday life, this means being careful whose advice you follow, whose approval you seek, and whose lifestyle you imitate. *Not everyone walking beside you is walking for you.*

On the other side lies the **danger of isolation**. Many people avoid relationships because of past betrayal, disappointment, or fear. But isolation leads to spiritual stagnation. God said from the beginning, "*It is not good for man to be alone*" **(Genesis 2:18)**. Isolation builds invisible walls around the heart. It cuts off encouragement, support, and correction—the very things needed for healthy growth. At work, isolation causes burnout. At home, it creates loneliness and misunderstandings. Spiritually, it opens the door for temptation, because in silence the enemy whispers lies like, "No one cares," or "You can handle this alone." *Temptation grows in darkness, but accountability grows in connection.*

In today's world, connecting with the right people is easier than ever. If you cannot find godly relationships nearby, pray and ask God to connect you with the right community online. I myself was completely alone in 2022. My only friends had left, and I refused to join wrong associations because I knew they could destroy everything. Instead, after praying for a year, God led me to an online community. Surprisingly, all of them were non-Christians, and I wondered why God had placed me there. But "My *ways higher than your ways, And My thoughts than your thoughts."* **(Isaiah 55:9)**, it became one of the best decisions for my overall growth. At the same time, I committed myself to **AMI (Alleluia Ministries International)** for spiritual growth. I encourage you to seek a community like this—an online prayer group and a professional group that helps you grow. But always remain prayerful and vigilant. **(1 Peter 5:8)**

While isolation is harmful, solitude is healthy when used correctly. Jesus often withdrew to pray, but He never disconnected from His disciples. The purpose makes the difference: solitude strengthens and restores; isolation weakens and drains. Use quiet moments for reflection, rest, and prayer—but return to your community for encouragement, guidance, and shared purpose. Every successful person, whether in faith or everyday life, understands this balance. They surround themselves with people who sharpen their vision, challenge their comfort zone, and keep them grounded.

The key to choosing relationships is discernment. Not everyone deserves access to your heart or your inner life. You can be friendly with many people, but close friendships should be built with those who follow godly principles. Whether building friendships at school, choosing colleagues to trust at work, or forming business partnerships, look for people who share your values and support your growth. ***Winning in life isn't just about avoiding bad company — it's about choosing the right company.*** The people around you should reflect the direction you want to go, not the distractions you want to escape.

The Reward of Godly Fellowship

Every good thing God wants us to enjoy—joy, peace, love, purpose—grows best in healthy relationships. Life becomes richer when we walk with people who share our faith, values, and vision. Godly fellowship is more than attending church; it is doing life together with people who encourage us, challenge us, and help us recognize

God's guidance in daily moments.

In today's world, independence and isolation are often praised, but godly fellowship reminds us that connection is our true strength. It fills the heart with joy, steadies the mind with peace, and supports steady spiritual growth. **Proverbs 13:20** says that "*He who walks with wise men will be wise, But the companion of fools will be destroyed.*" In the same way, those who surround themselves with people of faith grow stronger even in difficult seasons.

Joy is not found in material things or achievements–it comes from meaningful relationships. Life feels lighter when you have people who understand your spiritual journey, pray with you during struggles, and celebrate your victories. The peace you receive from godly fellowship does not come from avoiding problems but from knowing you are not facing them alone.

In practical life, this can look like a coworker praying with you before a client meeting, a group of friends studying together and sharing insights, or a family choosing grace instead of anger during conflict. Growth happens when people share ideas, correct each other in love, and encourage one another to stay committed to their goals and faith. Just as a plant grows stronger in good soil, believers grow faster when they are planted in a circle of godly fellowship.

Jesus gave His followers a powerful command: "*Love one another. By this everyone will know that you are My disciples.*" **(John 13:34–35)**. He also prayed that His people would be united, so the world would believe that He was sent by the Father **(John 17:21)**. Unity among believers is a living testimony that God is real.

When people see genuine unity in your workplace, family, or community, they notice something different—a peace and maturity that cannot be produced by human strength. In this way, Christian fellowship becomes evangelism without speaking a word. Unity also creates practical benefits: teams at work become more productive, families become more supportive, and entire communities grow more caring. When believers unite in love, gossip fades, cooperation grows, and the atmosphere becomes healthy for growth.

The reward of godly fellowship is not only what you receive—it is also what you give. A joyful believer spreads joy to others. A peaceful believer calms anxious hearts. A spiritually mature believer helps guide those who are beginning their journey. Fellowship creates a cycle of blessing that impacts entire communities.

When we walk together in love, faith, and purpose, we bring a glimpse of heaven into everyday life. The joy of one becomes encouragement for many, and the growth of the group becomes a testimony of God's goodness. In such a fellowship, we do not merely *survive life—we succeed* in it, together.

Chapter 9

Handling Setbacks: Growth Through Trials

Setbacks are a part of every journey, but they are not the end of the story. In God's plan, trials are not meant to break us—they are meant to shape us. Every delay, failure, or disappointment carries a lesson that prepares us for greater strength and maturity. This chapter explores how God uses difficult seasons to refine character, deepen faith, and redirect our steps. When viewed through a biblical lens, setbacks become stepping stones toward growth, not signs of defeat.

Biblical Perspective on Trials

Walking with God does not mean a life without difficulties. Instead, it gives difficulties a new meaning. James teaches that trials are not random events but God-allowed tests that grow our faith **(James 1:2–4)**. When faith is tested, it produces endurance, and endurance makes a believer mature, stable, and complete. Trials act like a furnace where shallow faith is refined into deep trust. Paul reminds us that God works all things together for the good of those who love Him **(Romans 8:28)**. That "good" is not always comfort or worldly success, but becoming more like Christ. Even painful seasons—failures, losses, and betrayals—are not wasted in God's hands. They can become building blocks rather than stumbling blocks.

Trials come for different reasons. Some happen because we live in a broken world. Some are the result of our own choices. Others are allowed by God as spiritual training. At times, setbacks expose unhealthy patterns like pride, fear, laziness, or the need for approval. At other times, trials are not punishment but preparation—God shaping us for responsibilities we cannot yet see. What matters most is not always knowing *why* something happened, but asking, "*What is God forming in me through this?*" Trials teach patience, dependence on God, and help remove false securities. When believers understand that trials have purpose, they stop seeing themselves as victims and begin to see themselves as students in God's workshop.

From a biblical view, a setback is often a hidden invitation. It invites growth in character, correction in direction, and deeper trust in God. Scripture encourages believers to seek wisdom during trials **(James 1:5)**. Instead of only asking, "*How can I escape this?*" we learn to ask, "*How can I grow through this?*" This change in thinking turns the same situation from a dead end into a doorway. The pain may still exist, but the heart becomes steady.

In everyday life, this means choosing to respond wisely rather than react emotionally. A delayed promotion can become a season to grow in excellence and humility. A broken relationship can teach forgiveness, communication, and healthy boundaries. A financial setback can lead to better discipline, stewardship, and trust in God. The trial may not become easy, but it becomes meaningful and productive.

Failure is often treated as the end, but in God's hands it becomes a teacher. The Bible shows that falling short does not disqualify a child of God. Failure reveals limits, exposes blind spots, and challenges wrong motives. When brought honestly before God, failure can lead to repentance, healing, and a wiser new beginning. Learning from failure means asking honest questions instead of hiding in shame. It also means separating identity from performance. A believer's worth is rooted in Christ—not in results, titles, or achievements. From this secure identity, mistakes can be faced without being crushed.

Failure can also act like a warning light. As I quoted **Dad Alph's** saying, *"Changing ways is always a sign of maximizing opportunities"*. Failure may signal that something needs adjustment—our methods, discipline, relationships, or timing. Instead of hearing failure say, "*You are not enough,*" a believer learns to hear it say, "*This approach needs wisdom and change.*" Sometimes failure is God's redirection. Closed doors, missed opportunities, or plans that fall apart may be God's protection or guidance. When surrendered to Him, even "no" or "not yet" can lead us to the right path.

Peter's life shows how failure and restoration work together. Confident and bold, Peter denied Jesus under pressure. His failure exposed the gap between self-confidence and true dependence on God. Yet after His resurrection, Jesus restored Peter with love and trust, not shame. Peter went on to become a strong leader in the early church. His story proves that serious failure does not have to be the final chapter. When met with humility and repentance, failure can produce a deeper and stronger calling.

Joseph's story shows how long seasons of setbacks can prepare a person for greatness. Betrayed by his brothers, sold into slavery, falsely accused, and forgotten in prison, Joseph faced repeated injustice. Yet he remained faithful in every place. God used those hidden years to shape his character and skills. In time, Joseph realized that what others meant for harm, God used for good **(Genesis 50:20)**. His life teaches that God's promotion comes after preparation—and preparation often happens through trials.

Therefore, when you face a setback or failure, do not panic or react quickly. Take time to reflect. Write down what happened, examine it honestly, and look for the root causes. Then bring it to God in prayer and ask what He is teaching you. We serve a speaking God, and He gives wisdom to those who seek Him. When you listen with a believing heart, even setbacks will begin to guide you forward.

For the past sixteen years (or more), I have been struggling physically with an incurable genetic condition. This progressive DNA disorder has made me wheelchair-bound since 2015. Even so, I continue to trust the God who heals—though the full manifestation of that healing is yet to appear. Over these years, I have endured many physical trials. My eyes required surgery. In 2021, my feet were operated on. In 2022, I experienced a financial betrayal from a close friend, which also led to another friend distancing themselves from me. Around the same time, I suffered a crack in my hip joint. In 2023, I faced another challenge when my eardrum developed a perforation. In **Dr. Lebo's** words, *"from cape to kero,"* my entire body has been affected. As a human being, I felt discouraged during those moments, yet through every season, I continued to trust God. I have been connected to the altar of AMI since 2022 (I used to attend services since 2019). I deeply desired to attend IVP, but each time, circumstances prevented it. This year, I sold my entire investment portfolio, obtained my visa and tickets, registered both myself and my caretaker for IVP (October IVP 2025), and reached the Mumbai airport. However, at the last moment, the airline denied boarding, citing the need for special medical clearance. Once again, I was unable to attend IVP, lost the money and felt stuck again.

These setbacks—and many others I have not mentioned—discouraged me for a time. But the God of peace, who guards the heart and mind, renewed my courage. Through every trial, He has been shaping and strengthening me. I have not been destroyed by these experiences; I have been forged by them. Today, I carry stories that testify to God's faithfulness. My life stands as evidence that even when healing seems delayed and answers seem distant, God remains present, faithful, and at work. I believe we are living in the end times, and in this dispensation, God will perform unimaginable and unbelievable miracles and I am one of those, for the glory of God. Therefore, I encourage you to view setbacks with a new perspective—what looks like delay or defeat today may be the very platform on which God reveals His power tomorrow.

Difficult Seasons Serve a Divine Purpose

Difficult seasons are not accidents; they are often part of God's preparation process. What feels painful today is often shaping us for future glory. The Bible repeatedly shows that before elevation comes testing, and before promotion comes preparation. God uses hard seasons to grow our faith, refine our character, and prepare us for what lies ahead.

A setback is never the whole story of your life—it is only a chapter. Every book has chapters that are difficult to read, but they are not the ending. God writes life in seasons. After a hard chapter, another chapter follows—one filled with clarity, restoration, and purpose, released in God's perfect time. When you understand this, you stop panicking in difficult seasons and start trusting the author and the finisher of your story. In 2021, I received a prophecy from my spiritual father that said, "*Your story with God is a golden story, and you are on the winning side of the story...*" That word gave me a completely new perspective on the '*difficult chapter*' I was walking through. I understood that for the later chapters of a winning story to be fulfilled, this difficult chapter also had to be part of the journey.

God often allows a "low season" to prepare us for a "high season." Before lifting someone, God works deeply within them. The low season teaches humility, discipline, and dependence on Him. It removes pride and builds endurance. Without this preparation, success can become dangerous instead of beneficial. As **Dad Alph** used to say, "***Capacity without character is dangerous***"

Even when it feels like God has left you in the low place, He is still working. Sometimes God needs to remove certain things, people, or mindsets before He can uplift you. Betrayal, rejection, and abandonment are painful, but they can also be purposeful. For many people, if others had not turned their backs on them, they would never have sought God so deeply. What felt like loss became the place where faith was born or strengthened.

True success is often built in hidden and painful moments, not in public celebration. As **Dad Alph** says, "*Success develops in the dark, not in the limelight.*" God sometimes places us in the shadows because that is where strength is formed. In loneliness, rejection, and silence, God shapes vision, resilience, and spiritual depth that cannot be developed in comfort.

Difficult seasons also reveal who is truly for you. God allows mockers, enemies, and fake friends to show their true nature. If you never go through a challenging season, false relationships can look genuine. As **Proverbs 19:4** says "*Wealth makes many friends, But the poor is separated from his friend.*" Hard times expose hearts. When the storm comes, some walk away—and their departure is also God's protection. It is said that, *'sometimes empty pocket buys precious friendship'*.

God also uses trials to purify and increase value. Just as gold is refined by fire, believers are refined through hardship. After the process, your value is not the same as before. You emerge wiser, stronger, and more grounded. What once shook you will no longer move you.

Hard times are not always meant to destroy you. Sometimes, they are necessary for your glory to be revealed. Just as labour pains come before birth, pain often precedes purpose. If a person is promoted without proper preparation, they may destroy what God gives them—just as a baby born prematurely may struggle to survive. ***The process protects the promise.***

Disappointment also teaches an important lesson: people are human, but God is faithful. When expectations from people fail, believers learn to place their trust fully in God. **Psalm 118:8** says, *"It is better to trust in the Lord than to put confidence in man."* This shift is painful but freeing. It builds a faith that is not dependent on circumstances or people.

Even the Church grows stronger through trials. Winds and waves test foundations, cleanse motives, and strengthen unity. What survives the storm emerges purer and more mature. The same is true for individuals.

Finally, God sometimes allows us to be broken on the inside so that He can rebuild us. *"The Lord is near to those who have a broken heart, and saves such as have a contrite spirit."* **(Psalm 34:18)**. A contrite spirit is precious to Him. In brokenness, God reshapes our desires, renews our mind, and aligns our fulfillment with His kingdom purpose. What He builds afterward is not just a better version of the old—you become new, formed by His heart and led by His Spirit.

Techniques for Handling Worry

Worries are often unavoidable, but they can hinder everything God has planned for us. The Bible says, *"Therefore do not worry about tomorrow..."* **(Matthew**

6:34). God would never command us to do something that is impossible for us to obey. This means worry and fear can be overcome. To overcome worry, we must learn how to deal with it wisely. Below are some practical techniques that people around the world—and I personally—use to handle worry and any emotions that contradict what God has spoken over our lives.

1. **Write it down**

   One practical way to handle worry is to write it down. When worries stay only in our minds, they feel confusing, heavy, and never-ending. Writing them on paper brings clarity. What once felt like a tangled mess becomes clear and visible. Once written, worries can be sorted. Ask simple questions: *Is this in my control? Is this something I need to act on? Or is this something only God can handle?* This practice can also become spiritual. You can write your worries in one column and write a Bible promise beside each one. In this way, the paper becomes like an altar—each concern is placed before God instead of being carried silently in the heart.

2. **Worry Handling Time**

   Another helpful technique is setting aside a specific "***worry handling time.***" This means choosing a fixed time each day or every two days—perhaps 15 or 20 minutes—to face worries intentionally. When anxious thoughts come during the day, gently tell yourself, "*I will think about this during my worry handling time,*" and return your focus to the present task. This trains the mind not to worry all day long. When the chosen time arrives, take out your list, pray over each concern, and decide if there is one small step you can take. Over time, worries stop controlling the whole day and become something that is prayed through and managed calmly. This approach is also helpful in families and marriages. Instead of reacting emotionally in the moment, couples can set an "***issue-handling time,***" perhaps in the evening or on the weekend, pray together, seek counsel if needed, and talk calmly. This strengthens relationships instead of damaging them.

3. Worry Tree

The "***worry tree***" method helps separate real problems from imagined ones. When a worry appears, first ask: "*Is this a real problem right now, or a 'what if?*'" If it is only a fear of the future or hypothetical, bring it to God in prayer and return your focus to the present moment. If it is a real issue, ask the next question: "*Is there something I can do about this today or this week?*" If yes, decide on one practical step—making a phone call, gathering information, setting a budget, or scheduling a meeting. If nothing can be done right now, release it to God again. This method helps stop the cycle of repeated worry and replaces it with either action or trust.

4. **Self-talk**

The Bible also teaches the power of godly self-talk. This is not a modern idea. In the Psalms, David often speaks to his own soul. In **Psalm 42:5**, he says, "*Why, my soul, are you downcast? Put your hope in God.*" In so many Psalms, David talks honestly to God about his pain, and then he speaks truth to himself. He reminds his heart of God's faithfulness and promises. This kind of self-talk is not pretending problems do not exist. It is choosing to align thoughts with God's truth instead of fear. It is preaching truth to your own heart.

Joshua may have practiced this. God commanded him to keep the Word on his lips, meditate on it day and night, and be strong and courageous

(Joshua 1:8–9). This required repeating God's promises to himself, especially when fear and responsibility felt overwhelming. Throughout Scripture, God's people strengthened themselves by remembering what God had done before. Today, godly self-talk may sound like: "*God has helped me before; He will help me again,*" or "*The Lord is my shepherd; I lack nothing.*" This does not deny reality—it anchors the heart in God's presence.

5. Balloon Method

Another helpful exercise is the "*balloon method.*" This uses imagination to release worries to God. Sit quietly and close your eyes. Imagine each worry as a balloon in your hands—one for finances, one for health, one for family, one for the future. Name each concern before God. Then, one by one, imagine opening your hands and letting each balloon rise into the sky. This represents surrendering that concern into God's care. This does not mean avoiding responsibility; practical steps still matter. But it is a way of saying, "*I release control and trust You with what I cannot manage.*" Many people feel physical and emotional relief through this exercise because the body and mind align with the spiritual act of casting cares on the Lord **(1 Peter 5:7).**

Handling worry does not mean never feeling anxious. It means learning how to respond when worry comes. By writing concerns down, setting structured times to address them, practicing godly self-talk, and surrendering control to God, believers learn to live with peace even in uncertain seasons. Worry may knock at the door, but faith decides whether it is invited in.

Emotional Coping Strategies

Emotional coping strategies help us partner with God in managing emotions instead of being controlled by them. People around the world use these practices because they are supported by neuroscience, and they also align well with biblical wisdom. God cares not only about our spirit but also about our mind and body. When we learn how to calm our emotions, we create space to hear God clearly and respond wisely.

Simple physical practices like deep breathing and mindfulness can quickly calm the body's stress response. Slow, ***deep breathing*** sends a message to the nervous system that 'we are not in danger, helping the heart rate slow down and muscles relax. ***Mindfulness,*** when practiced in a Christian way, means bringing our attention back to the present moment. Many times, anxiety pulls us into a '*fear of future*' or keeps us stuck in 'already happened past'—both of which are outside our control. By dwelling in these emotions, we cannot bring change, because God meets us in the present moment. Accepting the "now" and slowly repeating what the Word of God says about it can bring transformation. For example, during financial loss, you can repeat, "*The Lord is my shepherd; I lack nothing.*" In times of workplace conflict, you may repeat, "*The Lord is with me; who can be against me?*" This practice anchors both the mind and body in the present, where God's grace is active and available.

Another helpful practice is ***radical acceptance & surrender***. This means acknowledging reality as it is, not as we wish it were. It does not mean approving of pain, injustice, or suffering. It simply means refusing to live in denial or constant resistance to what cannot be changed right now. Emotionally, this reduces unnecessary suffering created by thoughts like, "*This should not be happening.*" For believers, radical acceptance closely reflects biblical surrender. Jesus in Gethsemane expressed His sufferings but ultimately prayed, "*Not my will, but Yours be done.*" Surrender is not giving up—it is trusting that God is still wise, present, and good even in difficult circumstances.

Opposite action is another effective strategy. It means doing the opposite of what unhelpful emotions are pushing us to do. When anxiety tells you to hide, the opposite action may be reaching out to a trusted friend. When anger urges you to react harshly, opposite action may be pausing, stepping away, or responding gently. When sadness tells you to withdraw completely, the opposite action may be taking a shower, stepping outside, or completing one small task. This aligns with Paul's words in **1 Corinthians 9:27** *"But I discipline my body and bring it into subjection..."* Emotions are not always reliable guides. Choosing the opposite action is a way of saying, *"My feelings are strong, but they do not control me."* Over time, these choices form healthier emotional patterns.

Caring for the body is also a spiritual responsibility. Exercise, rest, and proper sleep are not optional luxuries; they are part of stewardship. A tired body struggles to handle emotions well. Regular movement helps reduce stress, improves mood, and clears mental fog. Even simple habits like daily walks or light stretching can make a significant difference. Human beings need rest. When believers care for their physical health, they often notice improved emotional stability and focus.

Journaling is another powerful tool. Writing gives worry and emotion a place to go instead of looping endlessly in the mind. As I said in the last topic, One helpful practice is to write a worry on one side of the page and respond with a Scripture or prayer on the other. For example, you may write, *"I am afraid about finances,"* and respond with, *"You promised to supply all my needs,"* along with one practical step you can take. This turns journaling into a conversation with God rather than unproductive rumination.

Journaling can also be used to **record God's faithfulness**. Writing down moments when prayers were answered, help arrived, or peace was given creates a personal testimony of God's goodness. You can also record testimonies from others. I wrote down **Pastor Rodney**'s testimony of how God delivered him from armed robbers and preserved his life after a gunshot wound. Whenever fear of death tried to overwhelm me, I would read that testimony aloud. The Bible itself is a record of God's faithfulness. When we revisit these written reminders, our faith is strengthened, and our anxious hearts are reassured that the God who helped before is still with us today.

Faith-Based Methods

Prayer, Scripture meditation, and worship give strong spiritual grounding when life feels unstable. Prayer is not only a way to ask God for answers; it is a place to pour out confusion, fear, and disappointment before a loving Father who listens. Through honest prayer, believers move from carrying their burdens alone to placing them intentionally into God's hands.

Meditating on Scripture renews the mind by replacing fearful thoughts with God's truth. Instead of reading quickly, the believer slows down, repeats a verse, personalizes it, and allows it to speak into the current situation. Worship then lifts the heart beyond the problem. Singing worship songs like 'Show up, Jesus show up...' or speaking praise—even with tears—shifts focus from the size of the challenge to the greatness of God. Worship reminds us that God is still sovereign, still good, and still worthy of praise, even during setbacks.

As discussed in the previous chapter, accountability and support from a faith community are powerful tools for handling setbacks and staying strong. Christian faith is not meant to be lived in isolation, especially during difficult seasons. Seeking guidance from mature believers, pastors, or spiritual mentors brings clarity when emotions cloud judgment. Those who have walked with God longer can help separate truth from lies, wisdom from fear, and obedience from impulse.

The Bible clearly teaches believers to cast their burdens on God. **Psalm 55:22** and **1 Peter 5:7** invite us to give our worries to the Lord because He cares for us. This is not just a comforting verse—it is a practical action. Casting a burden means deliberately handing over what feels too heavy: fear about the future, shame over failure, or concern for loved ones. This can be done through simple prayer, such as, "*Lord, I give You this situation. I cannot carry or control it, but You can.*" Sometimes this act must be repeated many times. Each time, trust grows, and the heart learns that what feels unbearable belongs in God's hands.

Philippians 4:6 instructs believers, "*Be anxious for nothing, but in everything by prayer and supplication, with thanksgiving, let your requests be made known to God.*" The Bible does not say we will never feel anxious; it tells us what to do when anxiety comes. Prayer becomes the first response, not the last option. This habit can be practiced daily. When worry rises, it can immediately be turned into a short prayer: "*Lord, be with me in this meeting,*" or "*You see my child; please protect and guide them.*" Adding thanksgiving—thanking God for His past help and present presence—opens the heart to peace. God promises in verse 7 that His peace will guard the heart and mind, even when circumstances have not yet changed.

Scripture also reminds us that our problems are temporary. **2 Corinthians 4:18** teaches that "*...For the* *things which are seen are temporary, but the things which are not seen are eternal."* This means **every trouble has an expiry date. Psalm 30:5** says, "*Weeping may endure for a night, but joy comes in the morning."* These verses encourage believers to remain courageous and hopeful. Difficult seasons do not last forever. With faith, patience, and trust in God, every trial will pass, and joy will rise again.

Overcome Setbacks through Gratitude

Giving thanks during hardship is not denying pain; it is choosing to honor God's sovereignty. Paul writes in **1 Thessalonians 5:18**, "*In everything give thanks; for this is the will of God in Christ Jesus for you."* God remains worthy of praise regardless of outcomes. Even when loss feels heavy, gratitude shifts our focus from what is missing to what God has already provided. The food we eat, the shelter that protects us, the breath in our lungs—these are blessings that may be someone else's prayers. This shift moves the heart from despair to dependence on God. Over time, gratitude builds resilience. What may begin as difficult obedience slowly becomes genuine praise as we recognize God's faithfulness in unexpected ways. Trials lose much of their power when they are met with thanksgiving.

A simple and practical exercise can help develop this mindset. Take a pen and paper and write two lists: one for what you feel you have lost or failed at, and another for what you still have and what God has done for you in the past. You will often discover that the list of blessings is far longer than the list of problems. For example, if you are reading this book, it means you can see, read, and understand—many people cannot. You have time, awareness, and opportunity. This simple practice can shift your attitude and give you the momentum needed to begin again.

Gratitude also redirects attention from '*what you don't have*' to '*what you have*'. Losing a job may highlight missing income, but thanksgiving can reveal lessons learned, rest gained, or new doors that may soon open. Instead of focusing only on closed chapters, the believer begins to ask, "*Lord, what are You building here that I cannot yet see?*" This reflects the truth of **Romans 8:28**—that ***God works all things together for good***. When you intentionally remember past help, present comfort, and future hope, you train your heart to recognize God's hand even in chaos. Focusing only on loss leads to hopelessness; focusing on God's work leads to peace and purpose.

Another powerful step is reframing negative thoughts. Setbacks often produce lies like, "*I failed completely,*" or,

"This ruined everything." These thoughts can be replaced with truth: *"I learned important lessons,"* or, *"God can redeem this detour."* This is not false positivity; it is biblical thinking, aligned with **the renewal of the mind** described in **Romans 12:2**. The practice is simple: notice the thought, test it against Scripture, and restate it in prayer. Over time, this reshapes thinking patterns, reduces anxiety, and restores courage to move forward.

Celebrating small wins is another way to rebuild confidence after failure. **Zechariah 4:10** says *"For who has despised the day of small things? ..."* Progress does not always come in big breakthroughs. One focused hour, one honest conversation, or one completed task is still a victory. Thanking God for these small steps counters the '*all-or-nothing mindset*' that setbacks often create. You may even keep a "***wins jar,***" where you write down daily victories and revisit them during low moments. This habit strengthens resilience and proves that growth is happening, even when the journey feels slow. **Gratitude** creates momentum. It reminds us that God is still at work, that progress is possible, and that setbacks are not the end. When thanksgiving becomes a lifestyle, it turns discouragement into endurance and pain into purpose—helping believers rise again with renewed strength. Remember, '***Tough times do not last but tough people do***'

Chapter 10

Walking It Out – Discipline, Consistency, and Perseverance

Transformation is not formed in grand moments of inspiration, but in quiet, repeated choices made each day. It is through daily discipline that God patiently and faithfully reshapes a life. Small acts of obedience, practiced consistently, become the foundation for lasting change. This chapter explores how discipline, consistency, and perseverance turn faith into a lived experience and promises into reality.

The Power of Daily Discipline

Real change does not come only from a powerful sermon, a conference, or an emotional moment. Real change comes from what a person does the next morning—and the morning after that. Motivation rises and falls, but habits keep moving even when feelings are weak. When a believer repeatedly chooses to pray, read

God's Word, think rightly, and act according to truth, their inner life slowly begins to change. Over time, these daily choices reshape the mind, train the heart, and produce different results in everyday life.

Transformation usually does not happen through one dramatic event. It happens by renewing the mind and adjusting behavior one day at a time. Daily discipline works quietly, like water carving a riverbed. Each small action may seem insignificant on its own, but together they create deep and lasting change in a person's character.

Many people misunderstand the word "discipline." They associate it with harsh rules, pressure, or trying to earn God's approval. But for a believer, discipline is not punishment—it is cooperation with God. Discipline simply means arranging your life in a way that makes it easier to say "yes" to God and "no" to unhealthy desires. It is an expression of love, not legalism.

When a believer commits to healthy rhythms—such as spending time in Scripture, praying regularly, worshiping, journaling, working with excellence, or guarding their words—they are not trying to earn God's favor. They are responding to the grace already given through Christ. Discipline says, "Because I belong to You, Lord, I will shape my life around Your ways." This removes pressure and replaces it with joyful responsibility.

Big breakthroughs are often the result of many small, unseen choices. Exercising for twenty minutes once may not seem powerful, but doing it daily for a year can completely transform the body. Reading one chapter of the Bible each day may feel small, but over time it fills the mind with truth and pushes out lies. The same principle applies everywhere. Saving a small amount consistently builds financial stability. Sending one encouraging message a day strengthens relationships. Completing one important task with focus each day moves a dream forward.

These small actions are seeds. On any single day, they may not look impressive, but they are quietly building a future. When you understand that daily faithfulness multiplies over time, you stop despising small beginnings and start valuing each day as an investment in who you are becoming.

Most of life is lived in ordinary moments—commuting, working, studying, cooking, cleaning, and handling responsibilities. God often calls His people to obedience in these simple, unnoticed spaces. Obedience is not only about big decisions; it is about how you speak when you are tired, how you manage money when no one is watching, how you respond to irritation, and whether you work with integrity.

When a believer chooses obedience in these ordinary moments, the heart is trained. Obedience becomes a daily lifestyle instead of an occasional sacrifice. Over time, this quiet faithfulness builds a strong and stable life. Storms may still come, but the foundation remains firm because it was built one obedient day at a time.

In this way, daily discipline becomes the bridge between what God has promised and what the believer experiences. You do not need to wait for a special season to change. Every single day is an opportunity to walk it out.

Consistency Over Intensity

Consistency is the quiet power that turns good intentions into lasting change. Real transformation happens when a person keeps showing up regularly, even when there is no excitement or visible reward. Small, faithful actions done again and again build strength over time.

Emotional highs—such as a powerful sermon, an answered prayer, or a sudden breakthrough—can ignite passion, but they rarely sustain it. These moments feel strong, yet they often fade quickly. Consistency, however, builds steady momentum. A person who exercises intensely for a few days and then quits gains little, but someone who walks daily for months grows stronger. Spiritual growth works the same way. Occasional enthusiasm leads to ups and downs, but steady habits produce deep and lasting fruit. The Bible reflects this truth when it says the blessed person meditates on God's Word "*day and night*" **(Psalm 1:2)**. Growth comes from regular exposure to truth, not brief encounters.

Feelings can change, but commitment keeps a

believer anchored. There will be days when study feels dry, saving feels boring, or obedience feels heavy. On those days, consistency matters more than emotion. Choosing to show up honors God because it is based on trust, not feelings. Jesus prayed in Gethsemane during deep sorrow—not because it felt good, but because His relationship with the Father mattered. Over time, faithful obedience reshapes the heart, and joy begins to follow obedience rather than lead it.

God often builds character in quiet and unseen seasons. These are times of routine, delayed dreams, and unnoticed faithfulness. In Scripture, Noah built the ark for many years while being mocked, long before the rain came. In the same way, believers grow through daily work, study, eating healthy—even when no one notices. These hidden seasons develop endurance and strong faith. God values the process as much as the outcome, and He often uses invisibility to shape authenticity.

Consistency helps believers stay consistent. Simple structures—such as morning prayer, regular check-ins with accountability partners, or an evening gratitude habit—carry a person forward when motivation is low. Motivation may start the fire, but consistency keeps it burning. Daniel prayed three times a day even when it put his life at risk. His consistency sustained him in a difficult land. Practical steps can include pairing studying with daily routines, tracking progress for encouragement, and gently restarting after failure. When believers build consistency around God's Word and community, they move from glory to glory. Consistency may not feel dramatic, but it is powerful. Over time, steady obedience produces a life that is strong, rooted, and aligned with God's purpose.

Perseverance Through Resistance and Delay

Perseverance turns pressure into strength and builds deep, unbreakable faith. When resistance or delay comes, it does not mean God has abandoned the process. It often means growth is happening. Learning to endure teaches believers to trust God's timing, even when progress feels slow or invisible.

Growth almost always attracts opposition. When a believer chooses prayer, purity, generosity, or bold obedience, resistance often follows in the form of distractions, doubt, tiredness, or unexpected setbacks. Jesus warned that the path that leads to life is narrow and not easy **(Matthew 7:13–14)**. This resistance is not a sign of failure. In many cases, it confirms direction. Comfort often leads to stagnation, but resistance often signals that something best is being built.

Results usually take time to appear. Just like a seed buried in the ground looks lifeless before it sprouts, effort often shows no immediate reward. This waiting period tests faith and commitment. During such seasons, it helps to celebrate small victories—writing one page of the book God put in your heart, paying off one debt, or completing one step. Looking back at how God has helped in the past builds confidence for the present. Instead of worrying about distant outcomes, believers are encouraged to focus on today's assignment. As Paul wrote, *"I press on"* **(Philippians 3:12–14)**, choosing steady action over discouragement.

Delays also reveal where trust is placed. Abraham waited twenty-five years for the promise of Isaac, learning that God's "not yet" prepares the heart to carry the blessing. Job endured suffering he could not explain, yet declared, *"Though He slay me, yet will I trust Him"* **(Job 13:15)**. True trust releases personal timelines while remaining faithful during the waiting season. This waiting is not wasted time. God uses it to deepen prayer, strengthen character, and prepare believers for greater responsibility. God may not always shorten the process, but He always works through it.

Discouragement often whispers, "Quit," but perseverance responds, "Finish." Nehemiah faced ridicule, opposition, and exhaustion while rebuilding the walls of Jerusalem, yet he encouraged the people by saying, *"Do not grieve... for the joy of the Lord is your strength"* **(Nehemiah 8:10)**. Perseverance is strengthened by choosing praise instead of complaint, staying connected to a supportive community, and remembering that present struggles are temporary. Scripture reminds us that today's hardships are producing future glory **(2 Corinthians 4:17–18).**

Endurance is not based on human strength alone;

it is fuelled by God's grace. Those who persevere discover that God completes what He begins. As **Philippians 1:6** assures us, *"He who began a good work in you will complete it."* Through resistance and delay, believers are shaped into overcomers whose lives testify to God's faithfulness.

Finishing What God Started

Finishing strong honours God's work in your life and allows His full purpose to be revealed. God never starts something without intending to complete it, once **Dad Alph** preached over the subject of '**Alpha & Omega'** and taught us that Alpha who begins is Omega too who has completed the end, meaning The Lord never begins which He has not finished. However, He invites believers to walk with Him until that work is finished. When we keep our eyes fixed on Jesus, we learn to press forward as co-workers with God, refusing to give up halfway.

As mentioned earlier, God's faithfulness works together with our cooperation. **Philippians 1:6** assures us that *"He who began a good work in you will carry it on to completion until the day of Christ Jesus."* God initiates and sustains the work, but believers are not passive. Just like a farmer who plants seeds but must water, protect, and harvest, God supplies the power while calling us to daily obedience. When we persevere, God's promises unfold fully. Quitting interrupts the process, but faithfulness allows God's design to reach completion.

Staying committed becomes especially important when distractions arise. Life brings many distractions—new opportunities, comparison with others, tiredness, or unexpected crises. These can slowly pull attention away from what God has assigned. Paul faced hardship, opposition, and imprisonment, yet he said, "*Forgetting what is behind and straining toward what is ahead, I press on*" **(Philippians 3:13–14).** Commitment grows when believers learn to prioritize what truly matters, say "no" to good things in order to say "yes" to the best things, and regularly return to originality when focus is lost.

Life also unfolds in seasons. As dad says, the Kingdom of God operates in seasons and levels. There are seasons of preparation, growth, breakthrough, stewardship, and transition. Each season needs to be completed faithfully before the next begins. Recognizing when a season is ending often comes through prayer, wise counsel, inner peace, and visible fruit. Finishing seasons well—by learning lessons, giving thanks, and entrusting outcomes to God—builds spiritual maturity and prepares believers for what comes next.

The Bible compares life to a race. **Hebrews 12:1–2** says, "*Let us run with perseverance the race marked out for us, fixing our eyes on Jesus.*" This race is not about speed but endurance. Like long-distance runners, believers must learn to let go of unnecessary burdens such as sin, fear, or doubt. Scripture reminds us that many faithful men and women have run this race before us, encouraging us by their example. When believers run with focus, humility, and support from the community, they cross finish lines that matter—tasks completed, character shaped, and God's Kingdom advanced.

Finishing what God has started is an act of worship. Every step of perseverance carries eternal value. When believers choose to endure, they discover that nothing done in faith is ever wasted. God completes His work in those who refuse to give up, and their lives become living testimonies of His faithfulness. As Paul teaches in Ephesians 6:13 about *"having done all, to stand,"* Dad Alph has also shared deeper insight on '**Do All That It Takes**'. I encourage you to finish what God has begun in you and to walk faithfully in the calling He has given you.

As **Bishop Shepherd Gwenzi** says *'Livnoting'* or building, living as a builder (**LIVNOT**) every day means choosing to build with God in every moment of life. Each day becomes a construction site where morning routines lay the foundation, discipline and consistency add strength, a learning attitude builds a career, and the love of God shapes relationships. Small choices like kind words, honest work, and faithful habits etc. slowly build a strong and lasting life. Challenges and delays are not wasted; God uses them to strengthen the structure. When we build daily with God, we do not merely survive seasons—we leave a legacy that reflects His presence and purpose.

Final Words

I hope the pages you have read have helped you in your journey of growth. You have walked through this book not as a passive reader, but as a conqueror in preparation—equipped with God's Word, practical wisdom, and the unshakable truth that *greater is He who is in you than any challenge you face.*

LIVNOT is not the end of your story; it is the beginning of a new chapter. What you have learned—about setting God-aligned goals, stewarding time wisely, handling setbacks with faith, and growing through gratitude—forms a blueprint for victorious living. God has not called you to merely survive life, but to thrive in every season, reflecting His Kingdom through your choices, relationships, and daily habits.

Remember this: trials refine you, failures redirect you, and gratitude unlocks joy. You have learned how to cast your worries on God, how to see setbacks as opportunities for growth, and how to fix your eyes on what is eternal. These are not temporary techniques; they are lifelong rhythms rooted in Scripture. When practiced daily, God uses ordinary faithfulness to produce extraordinary transformation.

The principles shared in this book are spiritual, but how you apply them is up to you. There is no rigidity. You are free to adapt and practice them as the Spirit of God leads you personally. Growth is not about perfection—it is about obedience, consistency, and trust.

Today, step fully into your God-given calling to **build (LIVNOT) your life in Christ**. As Scripture declares,

"There is a time to break down, and ***a time to build"*** **(Ecclesiastes 3:3)**. This is your time to build. Surrender every remaining fear, doubt, and burden to Jesus—the ultimate Victor who has already won every battle on the cross. You do not fight for victory; you walk from victory.

Begin now. Choose one simple tool from these pages—a time to handle worry, a Scripture to meditate on, a gratitude journal—and apply it today. Share this journey with your community, walk with a mentor, or return to these chapters whenever you need clarity and strength. The Holy Spirit is your constant Guide; lean on Him.

You were born for this. Go forward and build—not by your own strength, but by the power of the One who makes all things new.

I am grateful to God and satisfied if, in any way, I have become a connecting dot in the life story you are building. Grace and peace be multiplied to you. The best chapters of your life are not behind you—they are just beginning.

Together for Life

Shalom

www.ingramcontent.com/pod-product-compliance
Ingram Content Group UK Ltd.
Pitfield, Milton Keynes, MK11 3LW, UK
UKHW021402190726
13845UKWH00028B/827

9 789356 195776